Where to CORNWALL

GW00359343

THE INFORMATIVE GUIDE TO EATING OUT IN CORNWALL

Editor: Jeff Evans
Art and Design: Lyndsey Blackburn, Sue Morgan
Editorial Assistant: Jackie Horne
Compilation: Martin Bale

CONTENTS

Cover Photograph: The Pandora Inn, Mylor Bridge, Falmouth
Tastes of Cornwall by Jackie Horne

Published by Kingsclere Publications Ltd.
Highfield House, 2 Highfield Avenue,
Newbury, Berkshire, RG14 5DS

Typeset by Wessex Press of Warminster Limited, Wiltshire
Printed by Blackfords of Cornwall
Produced through MRM Associates, Reading, Berkshire

Distributed in the UK by AA Publishing,
The Automobile Association,
Fanum House, Basingstoke, Hampshire, RG21 2EA

Foreword

David Mead

Foreword

by David Mead

Cornwall has always been renowned for its beaches, dramatic landscapes, cliff walks and wildlife, and recent investment in the county has added to an excellent track record in tourism.

Truro, for example, has now developed into a splendid centre from which to explore the county, and features the most highly-rated hotel in Cornwall (Alverton Manor).

I was honoured to be asked to provide the Foreword to this guide and I am sure that the increasingly discerning public can confidently use *Where to Eat* to discover the finer locations in the area in which to enjoy the full spectrum of cuisine, suiting all occasions and pockets.

I look forward to welcoming you to an area steeped in history, rich in hospitality and fully geared to tourism, and hope that this will be only the start of a long association with Cornwall and its finest restaurants.

David J Mead
General Manager, Alverton Manor, Truro

Preface

by Michael Warman, County Tourist Officer

W hat is it they say? We spend a third of our lives sleeping, and between an eighth and a tenth of our lives eating and/or drinking? It makes you think, doesn't it?

We plan our precious holidays with great care. We pennypinch over the rest of the year in order to live, for a week or so, in a style to which we would very much like to become accustomed. And when we get there — we sleep for a third of the time!

Michael Warman

But what about eating out? If it's true that we spend a considerable slice of our lives on this delectable pastime, shouldn't we plan our holiday culinary adventures with the same degree of care?

It is on this basis that I welcome this Cornwall edition of *Where to Eat*. It is surely indispensable in the preparation of a memorable holiday, and especially so when you have decided upon Cornwall as your No. 1 destination.

Cornwall, you see, is a land apart in any number of ways, and the culinary skills and regional dishes which flourish here are very much a part of the Cornwall experience. No Cornish holiday could be complete without a slice of seedy cake, sweet herb pie or Mousehole's famous Star Gazey pie (not to mention the ubiquitous pasty and — everybody's favourite — Cornish clotted cream).

Cornwall's seafood, it goes without saying, is second to none, and if the sound of pounding surf can complement the wine and ambience, so much the better. Good appetite!

MICHAEL WARMAN

Introduction

This *Where to Eat* guide has been compiled to offer readers a good cross-section of eating places in the area. We do not only concentrate on the most expensive or the 'most highly rated' but endeavour to provide details of establishments which cater for all tastes, styles, budgets and occasions. Readers may discover restaurants (formal and informal), pubs, wine bars, coffee shops and tearooms and we thank proprietors and managers for providing the factual information.

We do not intend to compete with the established 'gourmet guides'. *Where to Eat* gives the facts — opening hours and average prices — combined with a brief description of the establishment. We do not use symbols or ratings. *Where to Eat* simply sets the scene and allows you to make the choice.

We state whether an establishment is open for lunch or dinner and prices quoted are for an à la carte three course meal or a table d'hôte menu, including service, as well as an indication of the lowest priced wine. However, whilst we believe these details are correct, it is suggested that readers check, when making a reservation, that prices and other facts quoted meet their requirements.

Two indexes are included at the back of the guide so that readers can easily pinpoint an establishment or a town or village. We always advise readers to use these indexes as, occasionally, late changes can result in establishments not appearing in a strictly logical sequence.

We hope that *Where to Eat* will provide you with the basis for many intimate dinners, special family occasions, successful business lunches or, perhaps, just an informal snack. A mention of this guide when you book may prove worthwhile. Let us know how things turned out. We are always pleased to hear from readers, be it praise, recommendations or criticism. Mark your envelopes for the attention of 'The Editor, Where to Eat Series'. Our address is:

> Kingsclere Publications Ltd.
> Highfield House, 2 Highfield Avenue,
> Newbury, Berkshire, RG14 5DS.

We look forward to hearing from you. Don't forget, *Where to Eat* guides are now available for nearly every region of Britain, Ireland and the Channel Islands, each freshly researched and revised every year. If you're planning a holiday contact us for the relevant guide. Details are to be found within this book.

Chef's Choice

In each of our regional **Where to Eat** guides we ask an experienced chef, well respected in the area, to prepare one of his favourite menus:

*K*evin Viner, 31 years old, is joint proprietor, with his wife Jane, of Pennypots Restaurant in Blackwater. He began his career at the Royal Military Academy at Sandhurst where he worked as a civilian chef, serving meals to the military, politicians, the Royal Family and heads of state. In a subsequent seven years as teacher at the Army School of Catering in Aldershot he began to take an interest in culinary competition work. Since then he has amassed many medals, including seven golds at competitions in England, Europe and Canada. In 1988, as a member of the British team of chefs, he represented Britain in the World Culinary Olympics in Frankfurt. Competing against 29 other nations, the team won a gold medal and Kevin himself won a gold in an individual class.

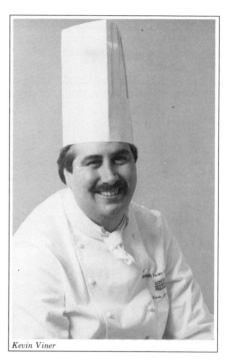

Kevin Viner

Here he reveals one of his personal selections of dishes.

"Being a chef, I can never learn enough about food. There is still so much to be discovered and I take every opportunity to eat out. I enjoy creating and cooking new dishes and eating at restaurants where the chef does the same, although I never go looking to criticise, more as a customer looking for a pleasant evening in a warm, relaxed atmosphere. I have set out here the sort of menu which makes such occasions so successful."

6

FIRST COURSE
Classic Consommé
A full bodied consommé made wholly from fresh ingredients with a rich flavour of beef and chicken. Garnished with a melody of vegetables, laced with sherry and served with hot crusty bread.

WINE
Petit Chablis
A full, deep fruit, firm and well balanced.

FISH COURSE
Poached Sole with Sautéed Shellfish
Poached sole and salmon plaits served with a shellfish and saffron sauce. Garnished with a lime and smoked salmon parcel.

WINE
Savennières (Clos du Papillon)
Dry and stylish with a velvety finish.

DESSERT
Chocolate Temptation
A chocolate, orange and Grand Marnier flavoured cream cheese dessert with kirsch and black cherries. Served on an almond chocolate biscuit with a black cherry sauce.

WINE
Coteaux du Layon
Delightful bouquet and light intense sweetness.

MAIN COURSE
Sautéed Breast of Duck
Duckling breast stuffed with spinach and duck liver, served with a Madeira, herb and champagne sauce.

WINE
Haut-Côte de Beaune
A firm fruit with a fine vintage.

Tastes of CORNWALL

Many people believe that food serves to nourish the body, but it also nourishes the mind. There has always been a strong connection between what people eat and their way of life, so that in the past when poverty, hunger and early death were commonplace, routine food habits were a source of security and special feasts could momentarily deflect the harsher realities of life.

Although each region of England shares a similarly based culture, it is climate and historical circumstance which primarily shape its cuisine. In today's environment, where high speed trains can link Cornwall to London in under three hours, and a uniform blanket of supermarket chains has spread over the country, it is hard to imagine the sense of individuality and remoteness once felt by the Cornish people, separated by the Tamar river and surrounded by the Atlantic. But in highlighting their culinary heritage, the Cornish spirit shines through and the past once again seems alive.

For centuries, writers like Andrew Borde, a commentator during the reign of Henry VIII, regarded Cornwall as a "Pore and very barren county of al maner thing except tyn and fsshe". Fishing was indeed a major source of the region's prosperity and also provided its staple diet. As the saying went, "Pilchards are food, money and light/ All in one night". During the season (which lasted from July to October), they were usually eaten raw, chopped up with onions and salt, or as Scroulers (dried on a stick, peppered and then cooked over the fire).

However, the most famous dish associated with pilchards, and one that is rarely seen nowadays is Star Gazey Pie, in which the pilchards' heads poke through the pastry lid, gazing up towards the stars. Although the heads themselves are inedible, they were not discarded because they contained valuable juices which would seep through the pie during cooking.

The pilchard season was followed by the herring season and then by the mackerel. With the transport revolution of the 19th century,

Cornish fish became much prized on the dinner tables of London, due to the fact that the cold waters from which it came produced firm flesh and strong flavours. Sauce was an important accompaniment. Saffron was often used to enhance the flavour of grilled fish which would have been too dry without it, and a rhubarb, or a gooseberry sauce was often served with mackerel, which needs a sharp sauce to balance the oiliness of the fish. Red mullet was another delicacy, usually prepared in a red wine sauce which added flavour, but which wasn't too strong to swamp the fish.

Shellfish was also a speciality and Port Navas still produces 25% of Britain's oysters. Mussels required much more elaborate cooking than their French counterparts (moules marinière) and were prepared with saffron and cider. Lobster was made to a recipe that dates back to Medieval times and comprises a rich pie of its meat, liquor and oysters. Towards the end of the 19th century the fishing industry started to decline and the population was often forced by necessity to eat coarse shellfish, or even seabirds and seals. Women scouring the beaches with an iron crook to twitch out sand eels were a common sight. Huge conger eels were difficult to catch, but it is said that they could sometimes be found lying helpless and bloated on the beach, having overfeasted from a wreck!

The diet of the poor was thus generally very sparse. Even in the days of large catches of pilchards, a salt tax meant that the populace couldn't afford to store them and had to waste them as manure. Most families subsisted on a diet of potatoes and barley bread, and gruel thickened with barley meal. Breakfast for many mining and farm families was a thin white slop of milk, sugar, cinnamon and currants, poured over a piece of bread, followed by Hoggan for lunch - a lump of heavy dough that occasionally contained a morsel of pork. Sunday lunch was the real treat when broth was served. This took the edge off a hungry appetite and was therefore particularly useful when there was no meat to follow. Kiddley Broth is another well known dish of marigold leaves, salt, pepper and butter, mixed with boiling water and poured over bread. Meat was invariably scarce and children had to make do with Scrolls (lumps of bacon fat) sold by the local butcher.

But, undoubtedly, the most famous Cornish dish of all is the Pasty, or

Tiddy Oggy as it was otherwise known. It was popular with mine workers because it could be dropped down a mine shaft and still not break and was always marked with the initials of its owner so that each Pasty could be separated by the workers at lunchtime, or if they had to leave it unfinished. The reputation of the

Pasty is widespread. The Devil himself refused to cross the Tamar, for fear of being made into 'Devilly Pie', and it is predominantly through pie making that the skill of Cornish chefs comes to the fore. In one respect, the Devil was right, for nothing has proved too large, or too small to be included in a pie, leading to some very unusual concoctions, including Squab Pie (made with pigeon, although mutton which tastes very similar is used today), Nattlin Pie (pigs' entrails), Giblet Pie (neck, liver and entrails of goose, commonly served at mine dinners) and Herby Pie (nettles, pepper-grass, parsley, mustard and spinach).

What distinguishes the Cornish pie from those of the rest of the country is its layer of cream, squirted in just below the crust, giving it its distinctive flavour. This was the most common use for the rich yield of milk which today is more likely to be found squeezed between a split, smothered in jam and eaten between sips of tea. Modern separating methods have altered the flavour of the cream, which was originally prepared by leaving the milk to stand for 12–24 hours and then slowly heating until a crust formed. Jam and tea were also largely unheard of; mugwort leaves were used to make drinks and thick black treacle to sweeten desserts. Thunder and Lightning (bread spread with clotted cream and treacle, and named after the frequent storms) was a popular dessert, as was junket, a mixture of milk, brandy and rennet. Children were told not to touch it whilst it was setting for fear of making it cry. Cream was also used to make butter, but, because it took a long time for enough to accumulate to sell at market, it was stored in a well. When it was retrieved, it would be covered in a slimy, grey film and unsuspecting customers had to be told that it was grey because it came from a grey cow!

The monotonous diet of fish and potatoes was, in part, relieved by the variety of cakes and fruit pies, available as a result of oven baking, the method of cooking preferred by Cornish wives. Figgy Obbin (a currant cake) and Saffron Cake were the most popular. How saffron came to be used so extensively by the Cornish has long been a heated debate. It still remains something of a mystery, but it is said that the Phoenicians traded it for tin in the 4th century.

Feast days regularly punctuated the year and were an integral part of day to day living, though, today, but for exceptions like the Helston Furry Dance and Padstow's Obby Oss, they have degenerated into mechanized fun fairs. They were always marked by the baking of cakes such as Revel Buns (made with saffron and clotted cream), and Wort Pie (made with whortleberries and eaten at the Triscombe Revel on the last Sunday of August). The parish of St Dennis is famous for the revolting tasting Sloe Pie, which was served up one year when the parish was short of money.

In Cornwall the birth of a child was also heralded, with the baking of a Groaning Cake (a reference to the mother's labour pains), followed by a Cheeld's Fuggan for the christening. A slice was given to the first person the family met on the way to church and, if they accepted it, it was believed that the child would avoid supernatural influences for the rest of its life.

Many blessings were also carried out, aiming to protect the harvest and ensure good crops. The Cornish, renowned heavy drinkers, were particularly concerned that the apple harvest should be a good one. On Twelfth Night (by the old calendar), 'Wassailing the Tree' is still carried out in Bodmin to frighten away evil spirits. Farm cider, or Scrumpy, more than any other drink, is associated with the West Country - innocent in taste and texture, but lethal in action. The old methods of production used nothing but pure juice and were anything but consistent in their final product. Frogs and fistfuls of earth, for example, were often added to aid fermentation.

Mead (honey-based and tasting of pure nectar) is another drink strongly associated with Cornwall and dates back to pre-Roman times. On the 24th August a blessing is carried out by the monks of Gulval at Mount's Bay. St Bartholomew, who heads their fraternity, is the patron saint of bee-keeping.

This tendency towards heavy drinking was reinforced by the Beer Act of 1830, which led to a proliferation of Kiddley Winks (inns), many of which remain today. The reformers hoped that, by providing ample beer, the populace would be weaned away from its preference for gin. However, in Cornwall, where the smuggling of contraband liquor was prevalent, the Kiddley Winks were as likely to sell the strong spirits as the cheap beer. Mahogany (two parts gin to one part treacle) was popular with fishermen because of its warming properties, as was Shenagrum (Jamaican rum, lemon, soft brown sugar and grated nutmeg added to a half-pint of beer). The name comes from a 16th century custom of reversing a glass until its last drop had fallen onto the thumbnail, thus signifying that the liquor wasn't shirked.

Many of those brought up to acquire the tastes of today's Cornish brewers like St Austell and Devenish would baulk at drinks like Eggy Ot (two beaten eggs and sugar added to a quart of hot beer).

Many complain about Cornish food; the pies are too heavy, the fish too oily and the cream too rich. But the food sustained a people who worked long hours under trying circumstances. The 'Delectable Duchy' and the 'English Riviera' would not have been terms used by previous generations of Cornish men and women whose motto was "A good strong stummick an' a-plenty o'work". It is, in fact, ironic that, with the decline of fishing and mining, the Cornish economy has been saved by a yearly influx of tourists who see in the landscape of Cornwall the golden hue of a past age before the countryside was decimated by motorways and office blocks!

Where to **Eat**

CORNWALL

Bedruthan Steps (Courtesy of the National Trust)

THE FALCON HOTEL

Falconbridge, Bude. Tel: (0288) 2005

Hours: *Open for morning coffee and dinner (last orders 9pm).*
                            Bar meals lunchtimes and evenings.
Average Prices: *A la Carte £12; Table d'Hôte £10; snacks from £1.*
Wines: *House wine £4.50 per litre.*

The oldest coaching house in North Cornwall, The Falcon was once the headquarters for the four-horse coaches which ran between Bideford, Clovelly, Bude, Boscastle, Tintagel and Newquay. Standing on this spot for nearly 200 years, it has developed a healthy reputation for hospitality, and is today run by Tim and Dorothy Browning, formerly Dorset farmers who moved here in 1985. With the help of their staff, particularly the chefs, the dining room (which overlooks the inner harbour), has a relaxing and intimate atmosphere. In candlelit surroundings, diners enjoy a menu based on French dishes, but with other international influences. Starters include scallops nantaise, and for main course there is fresh Cornish lobster straight from the sea. In the hotel bar Mexican dishes are very popular. Real ales too. Vegetarians and children have their own special menus.

The Falcon Hotel & Apartments, Bude

Tel: Management (0288) 2005 – Visitors 2382

14

THE VILLA RESTAURANT

9 The Strand, Bude. Tel: (0288) 4799

Hours: *Open for lunch and dinner (last orders 9pm).*
                    Closed Sun/Mon in winter.
Average Prices: *A la Carte £12.50; Sun lunch £6.25; snacks £1.50–7.50.*
Wines: *£4.95 per bottle.*

The Villa Restaurant has long been associated with visitors. It was built in 1726 as the seaside residence for Sir John Arscott, whose servant Black John, a 4ft hunchback, was the last court jester. Today Goff and Stephanie Walt cater for the yearly influx of tourists to Cornwall's northernmost resort with its renowned surfing beaches. At lunchtimes there are light snacks and meals available from the bar, whilst, in the evening, the à la carte restaurant menu contains a variety of international dishes including interesting vegetarian dishes like the vine leaves Roma (vine leaves stuffed with raisins, nuts, peppers, etc., served in a wine, tomato and herb sauce). Regular main courses include duckling with cherries in a port sauce, Angus fillet Villa (steak flambéed in brandy), chicken flotilla (chicken breast stuffed with prawns, lobster, cream and a butter sauce, cooked in breadcrumbs) and trout vermouth. These are matched by a fine selection of wines that Goff is particularly proud of, explaining taste and texture. The comment from one satisfied customer "I've added another belly to my ten already", says it all really.

The Villa Restaurant

The Villa · The Strand · Bude · North Cornwall

(Next Door to Nat. West Bank)

BRIDGE HOUSE RESTAURANT

2 Victoria Road, Camelford.
Tel: (0840) 212423

Hours: *Open for coffee, lunch and dinner. Closed Sun.*
Average Prices: A la Carte £13; Table d'Hôte £10; Sun lunch £5.50.
Wines: *House wine £4.75 per bottle.*

As the mystical seat of the knights of the Round Table and the site of Arthur's fiercest battle against the evil forces of Mordred, a place is notched in the history books for the ancient town of Camelot now Camelford. The town bestrides the River Camel, and The Bridge House Restaurant, itself over 400 years old, is a characterful place with low beaming, exposed local stone and a large open log fire. The menu can be neatly summed up by its motto — "What is patriotism, but the love of food one ate as a child?". Dishes are thus predominantly English, but with Continental touches. For a starter, try the duck, pear and bacon salad, served with mango chutney dressing, or melon filled with fresh orange segments and orange cognac. Main course options include fricassée of veal in a creamed coconut and fresh ginger sauce, baked seafood en croûte with monkfish, prawns, scampi, and scallops in a white wine and cream sauce, topped with puff pastry. Desserts are all home-made, change regularly and include the favourite mille-feuille and Pavlovas.

Bridge House Restaurant

Victoria Road
Camelford
Tel: 0840
212423

HEADLANDS

Port Gaverne, near Port Isaac. Tel: (0208) 880260
Hours: *Open for lunchtime bar snacks, tea and dinner.*
Average Prices: A la Carte £10.50; Sun lunch £5.75.
Wines: *House wine from £5.25 per bottle.*

Perched high on a cliff top, Headlands has magnificent views over the majestic and rugged Cornish coastline, as well as the tiny village of Port Gaverne. With Tintagel only six miles up the coast, this is very definitely the land of Arthurian legend, with even today the brooding landscape evoking his memory and sustaining the myth of old in the imagination. Villages like Port Gaverne, with their slate-hung cottages, still maintain an air of seclusion and the area is popular with those wishing to explore off the beaten track. There is little parochial about Headlands, however, since Anna Harris, the chef, comes from Poland and has spent many years catering in the Middle East. The menu reflects this international outlook and there are often speciality weeks. Popular dishes include teriyaki steaks and roast breast of duck in a redcurrant and ginger sauce. There are also plenty of local fish dishes, including crab and lobster for which Port Isaac is renowned, as well as dishes such as chicken in lobster and brandy sauce or home-made game pie. This family-run hotel encourages guests to linger over their meals, especially when one of the locally renowned sunsets can be seen from the windows.

HEADLANDS

Port Gaverne · Nr Port Isaac
Tel: Bodmin (0208) 880260

17

PORT GAVERNE HOTEL

Port Gaverne, near Port Isaac. Tel: (0208) 880244

Hours: *Open for morning coffee, lunch, afternoon tea and dinner (last orders 9.30pm). Closed Jan–late Feb.*

Average Prices: *A la Carte £14; Table d'Hôte £12; hot carvery Sun £4.75.*

Wines: *House wine £4.75 per bottle.*

The wild grandeur and solemn beauty of this stretch of the North Cornish coastline was succinctly expressed by Sir John Betjeman when he wrote "Here where the cliffs alone prevail/I stand exultant, neutral, free/And from the cushion of the gale/Behold a huge consoling sea". A sandy cove shelters the Port Gaverne Hotel, which has weathered the centuries since 1608, providing welcoming sustenance and hospitality with its 19 bedrooms, renowned dining and, more recently, several renovated self-catering cottages. The success of its cooking is based on a daily changed carte du jour and fresh produce from garden, farm and, more particularly, sea. From crêpes pêcheurs, through lobster thermidor to home-made Pavlova for dessert, a satisfying meal is the order of the day. For lighter meals there is a hot and cold buffet at lunchtime and bar snacks in the evening from the Captain's Cabin bar, atmospherically styled by a collection of antique photos, old oak chests and a marine chronometer. A warming bowl of crab soup, or Cornish fish pie is on offer to guests. Fred and Midge Ross are now celebrating 20 years at this family-run hotel.

PORT GAVERNE
HOTEL

★ We began our 21st year at Port Gaverne on 1st October 1988
★ Situated on a sheltered cove in an area of spectacular cliffs on the Cornish Heritage Coast
★ A staff who know how to care

NEAR PORT ISAAC, CORNWALL. Telephone: Bodmin (0208) 880244

ST MORITZ HOTEL & LAUREATES RESTAURANT

Trebetherick, near Wadebridge.
Tel: (0208) 862242

Hours: *Open for coffee, tea and dinner*
                (last orders 9.30pm).
Average Prices: *A la Carte £18; Table d'Hôte £14; Sun lunch £7.75.*
Wines: *House wine £5.50 per bottle.*

Trebetherick, according to Sir John Betjeman, was a place where "Roller unto roller curled / And thundered down the rocky bay". This area of flat, open beauty around the Camel estuary gave him his poetic inspiration and greatest joy.

    The 40-bedroomed St Moritz Hotel can be found at the estuary's mouth, near sheltered beaches, safe for bathing and sailing. It is a spacious place and the dining room, named in honour of the late Poet Laureate, is a credit to his name. The décor mixes soft browns and cream, and the cuisine, traditional French and English dishes: bouillabaisse, steak Café de Paris (tomatoes, onions, butter, herbs, egg yolks, wine and brandy), and duck roasted with apricot and brandy. The hotel also takes full advantage of the abundance of fresh, local fish, with, for example, coquilles St Jacques in a saffron sauce. A well chosen wine list accompanies.

St. Moritz Hotel

Trebetherick, Nr. Wadebridge
Tel: (0208) 862242

JANNER'S BISTRO

34 Molesworth Street, Wadebridge. Tel: (020 881) 2833

Hours: *Open for lunchtime functions and dinner (last orders 9.30pm). Closed Sun/Mon in winter.*

Average Prices: A la Carte £8.50; house wine £5.50 per bottle.

Jan Burridge has had over 30 years' experience in catering and built up a solid local following. Local stonework, a collection of jazz instruments and an altogether relaxing atmosphere partner a mixture of Continental and traditional dishes. Seafood pancakes and steak au poivre are preceded by 'boozer's mushrooms' and followed by home-made desserts.

The Gardens at Cotehele House (Courtesy of the National Trust)

GRIFFINS RESTAURANT at The St Enodoc Hotel

Rock, near Wadebridge. Tel: (0208) 863394

Hours: *Open for morning coffee, lunch, afternoon tea and dinner (last orders 9.30pm).*

Average Prices: *A la Carte £19; Table d'Hôte £12.50; snacks from £1.25.*

Wines: *House wine £5.25.*

Tucked away in a sheltered bay, three miles up the Camel estuary, The St Enodoc Hotel and Leisure Centre takes its name from one of the many Celtic saints who arrived here in the 5th century to Christianise the region. Today all manner of watersports are available, from lessons at the local sailing club to inshore or deep sea fishing. There is also squash or golf at a course containing the world's largest sand bunker. Alternatively, a quieter time can be had wandering around St Enodoc church, within the hotel's grounds. Once almost submerged in sand, it is now the burial place of Sir John Betjeman and reminiscent of his poems. The bias of the restaurant reflects its position by the sea. Dishes are cooked in a French style with coquilles St Jacques Mornay (scallops poached in white wine with a cheese sauce), and filet de boeuf aux huîtres et sauce bordelaise (beef fillet stuffed with oysters in a red wine sauce). Other meat dishes include carré d'agneau au sauce Cumberland (best end of lamb in a port and redcurrant jelly sauce), and faison rôti (roast pheasant with game chips and stuffing). Conferences are well catered for and there are bar snacks.

🌿 THE NATIONAL TRUST IN CORNWALL

Regional Office: Lanhydrock Park, Bodmin.
Tel: (0208) 74281

Hours: *Restaurants open for coffee, lunch and tea.*
Open Easter–Oct. Limited out of season opening, plus
events and functions.

Average Prices: Meals from around £5.50; snacks from around £2.25.

The heritage protected by The National Trust not only encompasses the monuments, countryside and shorelines of Cornwall, but also its cuisine. The traditions of regional home-cookery are nurtured and sustained by a string of refreshment rooms, to be found alongside the more grandiose buildings. Access and admission vary, however, so please check locally.

🌿 LANHYDROCK HOUSE

Bodmin. Tel: (0208) 74331

Situated at the heart of the Fowey valley, this 17th century Stuart mansion draws countless visitors to admire its ornate long gallery and landscaped gardens. The restaurants are appropriately situated in the servants' quarters, with seating for 120 people, serving cream teas, home-made soups, pies and flans. Licensed.

🌿 THE BARN at COTEHELE HOUSE

St Dominick, Saltash. Tel: (0579) 50652

Seat of the Earls of Mount Edgcumbe since 1485, Cotehele Manor, overlooking the River Tamar, is one of the most beautifully sited and best preserved late Medieval houses remaining in Britain, containing much of the original furnishings. The converted barn in the terraced grounds is now a restaurant serving a variety of hot and cold dishes. Licensed.

🌿 THE SAIL LOFT at ST MICHAEL'S MOUNT

Marazion. Tel: (0736) 710748

The little village of Marazion is dominated by the towering presence of St Michael's Mount across the water, reputedly part of the lost kingdom of Lyonesse. The Sail Loft above the National Trust shop specializes in freshly caught fish dishes such as the 'Hobblers' Choice' (an island ferryman's dish made with crab meat, mussels and mixed salad). Home-baked bread and desserts are also available. Licensed.

🌿 TRELISSICK GARDEN RESTAURANT

Trelissick, Feock, near Truro. Tel: (0872) 863486

The harmony of Trelissick with its surrounding views is widely renowned. Circling around the head of a small creek, which opens out onto the Carrick Roads anchorage, are gardens overflowing with exotic shrubs and plants. The National Trust restaurant can be found in a converted barn and serves savoury meat pies in a pipkin and farmhouse ham, as well as many home-baked cakes such as butterscotch flapjacks. Licensed.

TRERICE BARN RESTAURANT

St Newlyn East, Newquay. Tel: (0637) 879434

Standing opposite an Elizabethan manor house dating back to 1571, a converted barn now houses a pleasant restaurant serving morning coffee, light lunches and traditional afternoon teas. Licensed.

BEDRUTHAN STEPS CAFE

St Mawgan in Pydar. Tel: (0637) 860563

The cavernous rocks of The Bedruthan Steps — strewn along the coastline and jutting from it like jagged teeth — underscore the untamed grandeur and starkness of the Cornish coast. The café has been converted from the local mine buildings and serves morning coffee, light lunches and tea, accompanied by the like of lemon Madeira cake and cherry and walnut teabread. Unlicensed.

THE EDGCUMBE ARMS at COTEHELE QUAY

St Dominick, Saltash. Tel: (0579) 50024

A stretch of woodland, containing a chapel built by Richard Edgcumbe during the Wars of the Roses, separates Cotehele Quay from its manor house. Along the quayside, amid a row of 18th and 19th century houses, The National Trust refreshment rooms are sited in a former public house. They look out onto the Shamrock, the sole surviving stone carrying Tamar barge, and the River Tamar. Unlicensed.

St Michael's Mount (Photograph by Andrew Besley)

THE CARPENTERS ARMS

Metherell, near Callington. Tel: (0579) 50242

Hours: *Open for lunch and dinner (last orders 9.30pm).*

Average Prices: A la Carte £9.50; house wine £5.

Named after carpenters housed here whilst building nearby Cotehele Manor, the inn is enveloped in the atmosphere of the past. The bar menu is comprehensive, with pasta, pizzas, jacket potatoes and dishes such as navarin of lamb and beef bourguignon. Desserts include treacle tart, Carpenters' spicy pudding with brandy and cream and home-made blackcurrant cake. One mile off the A390 near Callington.

THE CARPENTERS ARMS

Metherell, Callington

Tel: (0579) 50242

THE EDGCUMBE ARMS

Cremyll, Torpoint. Tel: (0752) 822294

Hours: *Open for lunch, afternoon tea and dinner (last orders 9pm). Restaurant closed lunchtime.*

Average Prices: A la Carte £9; Sun lunch £4.95; snacks from 75p.

A mysterious and mischievous ghost haunts The Edgcumbe Arms, which has a commanding position overlooking the Plymouth Sound. Both locals and visitors using the ferry from Plymouth are attracted by its traditionally cooked food which includes dishes such as Tamar salmon en croûte, 'The Earl's Special' (succulently roasted pork) and chicken Kiev.

The Edgcumbe Arms

Cremyll   Torpoint

TALLAND BAY HOTEL

Talland-by-Looe. Tel: (0503) 72667

Hours: *Open for coffee, lunch, tea and dinner (last orders 9pm).
Bar meals lunchtime. Closed Jan.*

Average Prices: *A la Carte £17.50; Table d'Hôte £13; snacks from £1.50.*

Wines   *House wine £5 per bottle.*

The coastline of East Cornwall is dotted by tiny fishing villages and sweeping bays, many protected by The National Trust. The Talland Bay Hotel, framed by headland on both sides, has panoramic views out over the sea from the window seats of its bedrooms. Light oak panelling and classical cuisine mark the dining room, which also specializes in seafood. From the starter list select the lobster and snail cassoulet with hazelnuts in a green chartreuse and cream sauce, or locally caught scallops, stir-fried Chinese style in a black bean sauce. Main courses include a Cornish seafood extravaganza, with lobster, oysters, prawns and scampi in a creamy champagne sauce, lobster from the tank served in a variety of sauces and breast of free range chicken stuffed with Gruyère and asparagus spears, served in a herb and garlic sauce. Vegetarians are also catered for with dishes such as mushroom and hazelnut risotto. Filling snacks can be enjoyed from the bar and the summer barbecue served in the gardens is particularly popular.

Talland Bay Hotel and Restaurant

TALLAND-BY-LOOE   **TELEPHONE: POLPERRO (0503) 72667**
CORNWALL
AA ★★★ RAC — EGON RONAY RECOMMENDED

THE RUNNELSTONE

Buller Street, East Looe. Tel: (050 36) 2240
Hours: *Open for dinner (last orders 10pm). Closed Jan.*
Average Prices: A la Carte £12.50; house wine £6.45 per litre.

The 200-year-old Runnelstone is a typically Cornish cottage, but decorated with Middle Eastern touches. For a starter, try the hummus, followed by the 'Harpers Bizarre' for the main course. This is a gourmet selection of fresh local seafood (scallops, sole, plaice, squid, etc.), poached in white wine. There is also a tournedos gourmet (fillet stuffed with pâté, flamed in brandy and served on a croûton base with a wine sauce).

Looe

05036 - 2240

THE CELLAR WINE BAR & LOFT RESTAURANT

Quay Street, East Looe. Tel: (050 36) 2131
Hours: *Open for lunch and dinner (last orders 10pm).*
Closed Mon lunch. Bar meals available.
Average Prices: A la Carte £12; bar meals £1.60; wine £4.50.

Renovation at this 400-year-old smugglers' haunt unearthed bones and seashells once believed to ward off evil spirits. Low beams and enclosing stone walls still give the place a conspiratorial atmosphere. Local produce, especially seafish, makes up the blackboard menu which includes lobster and squid and dishes such as Hungarian goulash and home-made casseroles.

The Cellar Wine Bar
&
Loft
A La Carte Restaurant
THE QUAY · EAST LOOE
TEL. 2131

26

COUCH'S GREAT HOUSE

Saxon Bridge, Polperro. Tel: (0503) 72554

Hours: *Open for coffee, lunch and dinner*
                       (last orders 10pm). Closed Wed.

Average Prices: *A la Carte £15; Table d'Hôte £9.75.*

Wines: *House wine £5.95 per bottle.*

Steep cliffs crowd in around the tiny fishing village of Polperro, which more than any other epitomizes the Cornwall of the imagination. The fishermen's lime-washed stone cottages huddle together around the harbour, often standing sheer to the sea. Images of smugglers and of the King's preventative men who tried to thwart them spring readily to mind and are vividly portrayed in the novels of Arthur Quiller Couch, whose family lived at the Great House. The 350-year-old house still has all the atmosphere of an elegant gentleman's residence and provides dishes to match. Fish naturally plays a large part in the menu, whether as lobster bisque (garnished with cream and sherry) for a starter, or in dishes such as fruits of the sea (selected fish and shellfish in a cream and wine sauce) and monkfish provençale (sautéed with tomatoes, onion, oregano and garlic). Other dishes include tarsagnia chicken (a rich cream and vodka sauce, enhanced with prawns and lobster meat), garlic steak (topped with red wine, mushrooms and chopped garlic) and honey roast duckling. A selection of five vegetables is also included in the price.

Couch's Great House

XVII CENTURY
LICENSED RESTAURANT
POLPERRO

STAMPS

Bay Tree Hill, Liskeard. Tel: (0579) 48639

Hours:　　　　　　*Open for coffee, lunch and dinner (last orders 10pm).*
Closed Sunday.

Average Prices:　*A la Carte £17.50 (4 courses).*

Wines:　　　　　　*House wine £4 per half-litre.*

Stamps is situated in one of the oldest buildings in Liskeard — its former post office. A small market town set on a hill, Liskeard is characteristic of many lying in the wooded region near the Tamar river, which separates Cornwall from Devon. Beyond wrought iron gates and through a flagged courtyard, the restaurant can be found in a building with exposed beams. Whilst waiting for their orders, diners can admire paintings by local artists along the walls, or the collection of stamps. The menu contains many local fish dishes with Cornish crab soup as a starter, followed by local salmon poached in wine with a watercress sauce, or baked trout with hazelnuts and dill. There is also breast of chicken flamed in brandy with an apricot sauce, a range of steaks and fondue bourguignon (min. two persons), cubed rump cooked at the table and served with a selection of sauces. A well explained wine list accompanies the meal along with some traditionally produced alcohols — chauffé coeur spirits. There is also a cocktail bar for pre- or after-dinner drinks.

BAY TREE HILL　　　　　　　　　　　　　　　　**LISKEARD**

TREWITHEN RESTAURANT

3 Fore Street, Lostwithiel. Tel: (0208) 872373

Hours:	*Open for dinner (last orders 9.30pm).*
	Closed Sunday in summer and Sun/Mon in winter.
Average Prices:	*A la Carte £15.*
Wines:	*House wine £6.*

Lostwithiel, the Medieval capital of Cornwall, is the setting for the 300-year-old Trewithen Restaurant, situated near the old Duchy palace and River Fowey. The restaurant is now in its tenth year under the continuing ownership of Brian and Lorraine Rolls and offers quality, freshly produced cuisine. Mevagissey lobsters and local seafoods grace the tables in summer, along with prime sirloin and roasted duckling, whilst venison is popular in winter. The seasonally-changed menu is complemented by a daily blackboard and speciality evenings in which the chef's versatility comes to the fore. Here, experience gained working in exotic locations such as Bali, New Zealand and the Black Forest in Germany is exemplified in his imaginative dishes. A small, but well selected wine list accompanies, with premier crus from Bordeaux and Burgundy, some Australian vintages, Crianza Riojas and house wines from Tarn and Hérault. The service is friendly and unrushed, allowing diners to savour each course, and has helped make the Trewithen a popular restaurant with both locals and visitors alike.

TREWITHEN RESTAURANT

FORE ST · LOSTWITHIEL
CORNWALL

Reservations: (0208) 872373

29

THE ROYAL OAK

Duke Street, Lostwithiel. Tel: (0208) 872552

Hours: *Open for coffee, lunch and dinner (last orders 10pm).*
Bar meals available.

Average Prices: A la Carte £8.50; snacks from £1.80.

Wines: *House wine £4 per bottle.*

The hill-crested Norman castle of Restormel (the best preserved in the county), and the numerous Medieval buildings throughout the small town testify to the heyday of Lostwithiel's power and prestige during the 13th and 14th centuries. The Royal Oak, which also dates from this period, has an underground tunnel which reputedly links the wine cellar to the castle's dungeons and which would have been used as a smuggling route. Today the inn is well known for its hospitable atmosphere, real ales and home cooking. Snacks (including children's meals, freshly cut sandwiches, salads and curries) are available from the bar, whilst the restaurant serves dishes with a touch of France. Snails with garlic butter and French onion soup can both be found on the starter list, with treacle tart, apple pie and coffee ice cream with clotted cream for dessert. For the main dish, try some of the local fish, with, for example, lemon sole meunière, lobster and trout scallops, or, perhaps, sauté chicken in white wine. For vegetarians there are pancakes stuffed with spinach, almonds and carrots, coated in a white wine sauce.

THE ROYAL OAK
LOSTWITHIEL

Telephone:
BODMIN 872552

THE CHART ROOM

55 Esplanade, Fowey.
Tel: (072 683) 2367

Hours: *Open for dinner, except Monday (last bookings*
10.30pm), and Sunday lunch.
Average Prices: *A la Carte £13; Sunday lunch £5.75.*
Wines: *House wine £5.75 per litre.*

Old maps and navigation charts cover the walls of this harbour-front restaurant emphasizing Fowey's centuries-old connection with the sea. In Medieval times, for example, Fowey gallants regularly raided the French coast. Today, diners can linger over their meal watching the activity of the harbour below where yachts sail in and out, lifeboats are launched and ships from all over the world pass through to pick up the locally mined china clay which is turned into fine porcelain. The restaurant cooks in a traditional style with three set menus for the main course, but with diners choosing from a range of starters and desserts to fit each. Scrumpy lamb (a casserole with apples and cider) and lentil loaf are included on the Readymoney menu, whilst the Rope Walk menu features beef and walnut pie and devilled chicken. There are also steaks, local fish and lobster to be found on the St Catherine's menu and also a special children's menu. On Sunday a traditional roast is served.

Eileen and Robert Hatton

The Chart Room

Licensed Restaurant

Esplanade, Fowey. Tel. Fowey 2367

THE HAVEN

115 Par Green, Par. Tel: (072 681) 2417/4032

Hours   *Open for coffee, lunch, tea and dinner
(last orders 10pm). Closed Sun eve.*
Average Prices   *A la Carte £13; Sun lunch £4.55; house wine £4.40.*
Situated adjacent to Par beach, The Haven is a small and family-run
restaurant. Exposed beaming and dark tables contrast whitewashed
cobbled walls and red furnishings which are decorated to evoke a summer
poppy theme. The regularly-changed menu makes the most of local
seafood with, for example, crab claws in garlic butter for a starter, and
dishes such as Fowey trout in a buttered almond sauce for a main course.

115 PAR GREEN, PAR   Telephone: (072 681) 2417 / 4032

WYCH WAY INN

66 Eastcliffe Road, Par. Tel: (0726) 815601

Hours: *Open for coffee, lunch and dinner (last orders 10pm).*
Average Prices: *A la Carte £8.50; snacks from £1.50.*
The witches have their way only over the name of this characterful pub.
Eye of newt bubbling in the cauldron you won't find, but try the
'abracadabra' (grilled pork chop in an apple and mint glaze), or some of
'Merlin's magic' (veal steak topped with a fan of peaches). Amongst the
range of grills and fish dishes, a vegetarian offering can also be found,
with, for example, nut cutlets. Buffet bar and Sunday lunch.

THE WHITE HART HOTEL

Church Street, St Austell. Tel: (0726) 72100

Hours: *Open for coffee, lunch, tea and dinner*
                    (last orders 8.30pm). Bar meals.

Average Prices: *Table d'Hôte £8.50; Sun lunch £5.50; snacks from £2.*

Wines: *House wine £6 per carafe.*

The White Hart Hotel, formerly the 16th century home of the local squire, is one of the oldest remaining buildings in St Austell. It is also owned by the famous family brewery based in the town, although run for the last seven years by David and Christine Walker. 18 en suite bedrooms and the relaxing conference room have all been refurbished, with many of the rooms now containing original Nash watercolours. The dining room, decorated in pink, offers a traditional menu, with, for example, a White Hart cocktail to start (prawns and peaches blended in a cocktail sauce). The main course sees fresh fish including Fowey trout and Charlestown smoked mackerel, chicken, duck, a roast of the day and a range of steaks, like the Swiss steak in a tomato and celery sauce. Home-made sweets round off the meal. For a lighter meal, the bar provides a range of salads such as prawn, beef, cheese or ham, as well as a crusty home-made steak and kidney pie. Traditional British breakfasts are also served offering kippers and more.

Telephone: 72100
Guests 72827

Colour TV
Tea/Coffee
Accommodation

The WHITE HART HOTEL

ST. AUSTELL · CORNWALL

St. Austell Brewery · Est. 1851 · Independent Family Brewers

THE THIN END FOR HUNGRY PEOPLE

41a Fore Street, St Austell.
Tel: (0726) 75805

Hours: *Open for coffee, lunch and tea, 9am–5pm, Mon–Sat.*
Closed Sunday and Bank Holidays.

Average Prices: *Snacks/sandwiches from 50p; salads from £2.50.*

Wines: *House wine £5.50 per litre; 85p per glass.*

The traditional French style patisserie on the ground floor and coffee shop on the first floor are both friendly, lively and always busy. This is the case because Sue and Andy Ward who run them have so much to offer for hungry people. Hot jacket potatoes and crispy salads are available, but undoubtedly the highlights are the 19,600 sandwiches on offer, not to mention the cakes. A sample from the endless combinations are cream cheese, chives and garlic, anchovies, sultanas, bananas, peanut butter and stem ginger. For those daunted by the large selection there are some of Andy's specially prepared sandwiches with a combination of cottage cheese, pineapple and dates, or even toasted banana, honey and clotted cream. The gâteaux instantly ruin any diet, but are certainly worth it. Choose from devil's food cake, rum truffles, mocha gâteau, wild banana cake, rich fruit cake, or a beautiful fresh strawberry gâteau.

THE THIN END RESTAURANT and Pâtisserie

Open: 9-5, Mon-Sat

Fore Street · St Austell · 75805

HEWAS INN

Fore Street, Sticker, near St Austell. Tel: (0726) 73497

Hours: *Open for morning coffee, lunch and dinner
(last orders 9.30pm). Bar meals.*

Average Prices: A la Carte £6; snacks 65p–£2.25.

Built as a farmhouse circa 1600, The Hewas Inn (or 'summer farm' in English) has served the village of Sticker as an inn for nearly two centuries. The community atmosphere is very lively, especially at night when it is possible to dine outside under the illuminated flower display. A wide range of pub favourites — steak and kidney pie, moussaka and spaghetti bolognese, are enhanced by numerous local fish dishes and steaks.

Public Transport in Polperro (Courtesy of Sue Morgan)

TREGLOS HOTEL

Constantine Bay, near Padstow.
Tel: (0841) 520727

Hours: *Open for morning coffee, lunch, afternoon tea and dinner (last orders 9.30pm). Bar meals lunchtime. Closed Nov–Feb.*

Average Prices: *A la Carte £14.50; Table d'Hôte £12; snacks from £1.50.*

Wines: *House wine £4.75 per bottle.*

There is a strong contrast between the warmth emanating from the family-run Treglos Hotel and the starkness of the surrounding coastline. A golf course stands adjacent, running out onto open headland, and, to the right, the famous lighthouse and lifeboat station at Trevose Head. The hotel itself combines attention to detail with the personal atmosphere of home. A feeling of spaciousness throughout is enhanced in the restaurant by large picture windows which look out to the sea. The style of cooking is French and has gained a widespread reputation, particularly for the fish dishes. Lobsters and oysters can be chosen from the tank and many of the accompanying vegetables are home-grown. The cellar plays its part too, providing a wide cross-selection of wines to match individual dishes. Jacket and tie are requested for dinner, but the atmosphere is informal, particularly in the bar which serves snacks and lunches.

Treglos Hotel

AA ★ ★ ★ RAC

RECOMMENDED BY
EGON RONAY, SIGNPOST,
ASHLEY COURTENAY, B.T.A.,
AND DEREK JOHANSEN

45 en suite bedrooms

CONSTANTINE BAY
NR PADSTOW - CORNWALL
PL28 8JH

TELEPHONE - PADSTOW (0841) 520727 - 3 lines

Resident Proprietors: Ted and Barbara Barlow

THE BLUE LOBSTER RESTAURANT AT THE SHIPWRIGHTS

North Quay, Padstow. Tel: (0841) 532451

Hours: *Open for dinner. Bar meals available.*

Average Prices: A la Carte £13.50; Table d'Hôte £10.95; snacks from £1.

Wines   *House wine £4.50 per bottle (table over four receive a complimentary bottle).*

The small town of Padstow, mercifully spared the full rigours of the tourist trade, is characterised by a mass of winding streets. The harbour has also retained its character and is still crowded with local fishermen. Large ships cannot enter because, according to legend, a mermaid silted up the estuary in anger at being shot at. Catches of lobster, prawns and crab are brought through daily, however, and provide the staple dishes on the two menus at The Shipwrights. The pub itself serves light meals and traditional snacks, with home-made curries, fishermen's lunches, steak and kidney pie and various fresh salads with home-cooked meats. Real ales too. Upstairs, the restaurant, decorated in kingfisher blue, serves a range of international dishes accompanied by fresh vegetables. Baked scallops in a cheese sauce, or king prawns in garlic butter for a starter, could be followed by scampi oriental, fresh salmon in champagne sauce, or perhaps, steak Diane. Home-made sweets round off the meal, which is accompanied by a comprehensive wine list.

THE BLUE LOBSTER AT THE SHIPWRIGHTS.   NORTH QUAY, PADSTOW. Tel: (0841) 532451

THE OLD CUSTOM HOUSE INN

South Quay, Padstow.
Tel: (0841) 532359

Hours: *Open for coffee, lunch and dinner (last orders 9.30pm).*
                    Closed Nov–March.
Average Prices: *A la Carte £14; Table d'Hôte £11.95; snacks from £2.*
Wines: *House wine £3.25 per bottle.*

Until the late 19th century, the Georgian Custom House and its adjoining warehouse played a key role in the Padstow economy, geared heavily towards smuggling as well as the staple industry of fishing. The Custom House, which stood on the beach until a jetty was built in 1910, now houses a comfortable hotel and restaurant. Fish is naturally a speciality and, since the hotel owns its own trawler, 'The Flamingo', freshness is assured. To begin a meal here, start with a crab terrine (pâté served with an avocado sauce), or, perhaps, a fresh melon buée (blueberry sauce). The main course changes regularly, but there is always a fish dish of the day and a selection of seafoods cooked in a tomato sauce with pasta. Other typical dishes include noisettes of lamb with garlic and rosemary, char-grilled chicken breast with a cushion of fresh vegetables and, for dessert, a brandy snap basket filled with apple and ginger ice cream, garnished with fresh apple. Bar meals are also available.

• THE OLD CUSTOM HOUSE •

PADSTOW, NORTH CORNWALL   *Tel: (0841) 532359*

ST BENET'S ABBEY HOTEL AND RESTAURANT

Truro Road, Lanivet, near Bodmin. Tel: (0208) 831352
Hours: *Open for coffee, lunch, tea and dinner (last orders 10pm).*
Average Prices: A la Carte £17; Table d'Hôte £10.50; Sun lunch £8.

Built in 1411 to serve as a hospital, St Benet's Abbey later became home to the powerful Courtenay family. Today a gothic atmosphere still prevails, as do parts of the original house and chapel. The restaurant itself serves an array of traditional, French and nouvelle cuisine dishes with, for example, lamb steak Beau Nash, veal Orloff and chateaubriand. Accompanying at each end of the menu are dishes such as moules marinière and a fruit terrine.

15th CENTURY ST. BENET'S ABBEY

a Cornish retreat
known for good food
and
comfort with service

LANIVET, Nr. BODMIN
Telephone: (0208) 831352

THE OLD RECTORY HOTEL AND COUNTRY CLUB

St Columb. Tel: (0637) 881310
Hours: *Open for lunch and dinner (last orders 10pm).*
Bar meals lunchtime. Closed Mon/Tues.
Average Prices: A la Carte £18; Table d'Hôte £8.75; Sun lunch £5.75.

Built in 1288, The Old Rectory is surrounded by a moat and a garden full of rhododendrons. Within, stained glass windows and carved stone abound. Light lunches are served in the chapel bistro, and imaginative cuisine in the restaurant with its high vaulted ceiling and minstrel's gallery. Smoked trout from a stream in the grounds and lemon and pork fillets with chicory in a Brie and Dijon mustard sauce are just two choices available.

The Old Rectory

A Restaurant with Rooms

ST. COLUMB MAJOR
CORNWALL

Telephone:
St. Columb (0637) 881310

THE LANHERNE PUB

32 Ulalia Road, Newquay.
Tel: (0637) 872308

Hours: *Open for coffee, lunch and dinner (last orders 9.30pm).*
Bar meals available.
Average Prices: *A la Carte £10.50; Sun lunch £4.95; bar meals from £1.75.*
Wines: *House wine £5.50 per bottle.*

The Lanherne successfully fuses an unusual combination of styles. The bar has all the atmosphere of a local, serving real ales and traditional snacks, whilst the dining room has a distinctive and airy, pre-war, colonial feel to it. Meticulously laid tables are bordered by touches of greenery, carefully hung miniatures, ornately styled windows and mirrors, and swishing fans on the ceiling. The service matches the atmosphere — smart, but relaxed and has proved particularly popular with businessmen at lunchtime.

From the à la carte menu choose, perhaps, scooped melon balls soaked in port, or whitebait served with tartare sauce. For the main course, chicken, lamb and steak dishes are accompanied by a range of sauces, including chasseur sauce, garlic butter sauce, barbecue sauce and sauce au poivre. There are also dishes such as chicken Kiev, fresh trout and lobster, subject to availability. For dessert, try the hot Belgium apple pie with custard, or a chocolate nut sundae comprising chocolate ice cream and sauce, fresh cream, chopped nuts and a wafer. Accommodation is also available.

THE
LANHERNE
PUB
A LA CARTE RESTAURANT
Tel. 0637 872308

THE RIF RESTAURANT

20 East Street, Newquay.
Tel: (0637) 872964

Hours: Open for breakfast, morning coffee, lunch,
                    afternoon tea and dinner. Closed Nov–Feb.
Average Prices: A la Carte £5; snacks from 80p.
Wines: £5 per bottle; 85p per glass.

The Rif mountains of Morocco, after which this restaurant is named, are a far cry from the sandy beaches and Atlantic rollers of Newquay. As Cornwall's premier tourist resort, it attracts many families who can participate in all manner of activities including deep sea shark fishing. It is towards families that the restaurant is geared with a menu ranging from full English breakfasts to Cornish cream teas and full à la carte meals. Both can be taken either in the casual eating bar or upstairs in the restaurant. Recently refurbished, the restaurant is decorated throughout in green with stained oak veneer tables, bent wood chairs and a pine pitched ceiling. Good value, freshly prepared food is their hallmark with a range of eight grills, omelettes, pizzas, stuffed jacket potatoes and salads that sit side by side with duck à l'orange, roast beef, sirloin steak and chilli con carne. Chicken nuggets and fish fingers will please the children, as will the long dessert list which includes hot chocolate fudge cake with ice cream, apple crumble, fresh cream doughnuts and knickerbocker glories.

The Rif Restaurant, 20 East Street, Newquay. Tel: (0637) 872964

STAR RATING
FOR CORNWALL'S TOP HOTEL RESTAURANT

The Terrace Restaurant of Truro's Alverton Manor Hotel has just been awarded an Egon Ronay Star. At the same time the hotel itself has achieved a 75% rating in the 1988 Egon Ronay/Cellnet Guide, the highest rating of any hotel in the County.

Alverton Manor's achievement is made even more remarkable by the fact that the Egon Ronay representatives visited the hotel barely seven months after it was opened. For any hotel and restaurant the Egon Ronay accolade represents a pinnacle of professionalism and refinement. For that to be achieved in such a short time is a rare achievement indeed.

Alverton Manor, already listed in The Good Food Guide, and with a Dairy Crest 'Outstanding Cheeseboard' award to its credit is now more than justified in its claim to be Cornwall's Premier Hotel.

NEW FOR 1989

January 1989 sees the opening of Alverton Manor's second Restaurant.

Known as the 'Oak Room' it will offer a full range of dishes, featuring the finest produce. Guests will be welcomed with a choice of two or three courses including house specialities and vegetarian dishes, combined with a menu reflecting the traditional 'Grill Room' style of cuisine.

TREGOLLS ROAD · TRURO · CORNWALL · TR1 1XQ
TELEPHONE: (0872) 76633 · FAX: (0872) 222989

42

ALVERTON MANOR

Tregolls Road, Truro.
Tel: (0872) 76633

Hours:	*Open for coffee, lunch, tea and dinner.*
Average Prices:	*A la Carte £23.*
Wines:	*House wine £7.75.*

Alverton Manor carries in its atmosphere the certainty of age. A grade II listed building, once occupied by the sisters of Epiphany, and built to a rambling Gothic style with mullioned windows and gabled arches encased in sandstone walls, it gives a lasting impression of a Medieval relic hidden for centuries within its six acres of grounds. Inside, the hotel has all the hallmarks of grand country living, a feat carefully contrived by the owners, Maureen and James Costelloe. Formal tie-back curtains with extravagant ruches accompany elegant furnishings that blend harmoniously into the background suggesting an air of relaxing serenity.

This is a perfect backdrop to the highly acclaimed cuisine of chef Alan Vickops who previously worked at The Dorchester in London. The style is English nouvelle cuisine: dishes are imaginatively presented and meticulously crafted so that light sauces do not swamp the food, but bring out its true flavour.

For an appetizer there is a pot pourri of smoked salmons with a tossed green bean leaf salad, a brioche of scallops and crispy bacon in a nest of various leaves with a walnut oil dressing, and a wild mushroom terrine with a lemon dressing scented with dill weed.

In line with many quality restaurants, the choice for the main course is not extensive, but the menu is carefully composed to include a range of different dishes. Fillet of brill topped with baked aubergine and wrapped in spinach leaves, served on a pool of Pernod with a dill butter sauce, and a pot pourri of Cornish seafish served with a Madeira and truffle butter sauce are two of the available fish choices. For a poultry dish there is honey and herb roasted duck breast served on a pink peppercorn and ginger sauce; for a game dish, venison medallion sitting on a rösti potato cake with a rich orange sauce and caramelised citron zest, and, for a beef dish, baked Scotch fillet with cream braised mushrooms and a red wine and rosemary sauce.

Finally, there are the delicate desserts with, for example, white chocolate swans on a pool of dark chocolate sauce, hot apple soufflé with a calvados sauce, or an iced coffee and coconut parfait layered with hazelnut meringue on a pool of vanilla sauce. The meal is then completed with freshly brewed coffee and home-made petits fours.

THE GANGES

St Clement Street, Truro. Tel: (0872) 42535

Hours: *Open for lunch and dinner*
(last orders 11.15pm Sun–Thurs, 11.45pm Fri/Sat).

Average Prices: A la Carte £12–16.

Wines: *House wine £5.95 per bottle.*

Sister branch to the Ganges Restaurant in Penzance, the Truro tandoori specializes in the same high quality classical Indian cuisine. Indian chefs pride themselves on their skilfulness in the blending and preparation of spices to create the distinctive and aromatic flavours found in their dishes. They are as meticulous about detail, and as dedicated to the task, as the French are with their sauces. The chefs at The Ganges are no exception. Typical of their dishes are lamb Jaipuri (diced meat cooked in yoghurt, mildly spiced and served with egg) and chicken moglai (mildly spiced, cooked with cream and yoghurt and garnished with almonds). The house specialities are even more elaborate. The tandoori mix comprises tandoori chicken, chicken tikka, seekh kebab, tikka kebab and nan. Two people can enjoy the tandoori murghee masala (prawn bhoona and puri, and tandoori chicken in special spices), whilst, for four people, there is kursi lamb (leg of lamb marinated and roasted with ground spices and a variety of herbs). The special preparation of this dish requires 24 hours' notice.

The Ganges Indian Restaurant, St Clement Street, Truro. Tel: (0872) 42535

THE WILLIAM IV

Kenwyn Street, Truro. Tel: (0872) 73334
Hours: Open 11am–11pm (12–3pm and 7–10.30pm Sun).
Average Prices: Meals from £2.50; snacks 85p.

William IV is one of Britain's least remembered monarchs, but it is an appropriate name for a pub in Truro, reflecting the city's most prosperous era during the late 18th and early 19th centuries when it rivalled Bath as one of the leading cultural centres in Britain. The atmosphere within the pub has a distinct Victorian air, enhanced by the recent addition of a conservatory and an award winning garden. The 20th century asserts itself, however, through a big screen video and satellite television installation, which enable pop videos and screen sports to be shown. A comprehensive range of traditional bar food is served with wholemeal sandwiches, omelettes, burgers, toasted sandwiches and filled jacket potatoes. The fillings for the latter include ham and sweetcorn, onion and chive, and prawns. There is also a range of fresh salads accompanied by dishes of roast beef, turkey and ham, farmhouse pie, vegetarian quiche and egg mayonnaise and asparagus. Those seeking a hot meal have a choice between traditional home-cooked dishes such as fish pie, vegetarian crumble or ham, leek and potato hot pot. As well as curries and casseroles there are pasties and pies, platters and fries. The combination of the conservatory and light meals has proved particularly popular.

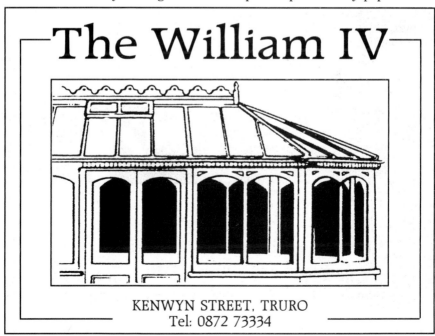

The William IV

KENWYN STREET, TRURO
Tel: 0872 73334

APPLEJACKS

19 Old Bridge Street, Truro. Tel: (0872) 73800

Hours: *Open for coffee, lunch, tea and dinner.*

Average Prices: A la Carte £8; house wine £5.25 per bottle.

Situated near Truro's Victorian cathedral, Applejacks occupies a waterside position and has a terrace overlooking the river. Within, a bistro décor and atmosphere is matched by similarly styled cuisine, simply cooked in generous proportions. The chicken Kiev is particularly popular, but other dishes include chilli con carne, chicken and apricot curry and vegetable lasagne. There is also a range of salads and jacket potatoes.

Applejacks

Restaurant & Wine Bar
19 Old Bridge Street, Truro.
Telephone: Truro 73800

THE PEACOCK COTTAGE HOTEL
AND RESTAURANT

Threemilestone, Truro. Tel: (0872) 78479

Hours: *Open for lunch and dinner. Closed Sat lunch and Sun.*

Average Prices: A la Carte £12; snacks from £1.50.

A huge log fire adds to the cottagey atmosphere of this traditional Cornish restaurant. Try the minted green pea soup with croûtons for a starter, or the poached scallops. For the main course there is a selection from the grill, or dishes such as breast of duck with a bramble sauce and sautéed pork fillet in a cider and calvados sauce. Crème brûlée concludes.

The Peacock
Cottage
Restaurant
Threemilestone

Philip and Cherida welcome you to dine at the restaurant with the cottage feel and character and in a friendly homely atmosphere.

Choose from a wide and varied selection of freshly cooked dishes.

THE LUGGER HOTEL AND RESTAURANT

Portloe, near Truro. Tel: (0872) 501322

Hours: *Open for coffee, light lunches, tea and dinner. Closed mid Nov–mid March.*

Average Prices: A la Carte £15; Table d'Hôte £11.95; Sun lunch £6.95; snacks from £1. House wine £3.75 per carafe.

Situated at the very water's edge of the small fishing cove of Portloe, The Lugger Hotel has been serving the community since the 17th century — first as a smuggling inn and for the last 40 years as a hotel under the Powell family. Its dining room serves a selection of English and Continental dishes from its table d'hôte and à la carte menus. Three coloured melon (marinated pearls of melon in kirsch, Grand Marnier and crème de menthe) makes an interesting start to a meal. Following on to the main course, fish is naturally a speciality, with dishes such as plaice Cecilia (topped with asparagus spears and melted cheese), and scallops in bacon and brandy. Other dishes include duck Sumatra (trimmed with stem ginger and almonds in a honey, lemon and white wine sauce), and, for vegetarians, dishes such as macaroni savoury (bound with a white wine and cheese sauce, baked and served with a spicy tomato sauce). Cornish ice and clotted creams are used to produce desserts like ginger · butterscotch supreme amongst others. Bar meals are also available.

The Lugger & Hotel RESTAURANT

Portloe, Nr. Truro, Cornwall.   Telephone: (0872) 501322

IDLE ROCKS HOTEL

Tredenham Road, St Mawes. Tel: (0326) 270771

Hours:	*Open for coffee, lunch, tea and dinner (last orders 9.15pm). Closed Jan/Feb. Bar meals lunchtime.*
Average Prices:	*A la Carte £14.50; Table d'Hôte £15; snacks from £1.50.*
Wines:	*House wine £6 per bottle.*

Lying across the Carrick Roads from neighbouring Falmouth, St Mawes is a mirror image in miniature — a small and extremely popular yachting centre moored at the tip of the Roseland peninsula. The Idle Rocks Hotel lies on the sheltered waterfront and its Terrace Restaurant has views that stretch right out over the sea. Within, a huge watercolour by local artist Chas Pears shadows the dining room, which offers a mixture of traditional French and English cuisine from its chef Keith Ives. His dishes are an interesting combination of seasonal fruits and vegetables. Commencing with the starters, diners may find slices of chilled melon with a raspberry coulis and smoked salmon with a compote of pears. For the main course there is roast guinea fowl in a blackberry and Drambuie sauce, escalope of veal with a mushroom, pineapple and ginger wine sauce, and breast of chicken topped with a fresh fruit and Tia Maria sauce. Desserts are not neglected either, with, for example, strawberry and kiwi Pavlova, blackberry pancakes and 'Death by Chocolate' gâteau.

Idle Rocks Hotel

KEA HOUSE RESTAURANT

69 Fore Street, Tregony, Truro. Tel: (087 253) 642.

Hours: *Open for dinner all year and coffee, lunch and cream teas in summer. Closed Sunday.*

Average Prices: *A la Carte £12.50.*

Wines: *House wine £4.75 per bottle.*

After many years' catering North of the Border, Ann and Alex Nixon, the proprietors of Kea House, have brought Scottish flair and enthusiasm to Cornwall. The friendly welcome diners receive is complemented by an appetising menu of carefully prepared, seasonally based, traditional dishes. Begin with Scots haggis and a 'taste o'Glen Morangie', or, perhaps, the more local Mevagissey crêpe stuffed with freshly caught seafood. Main courses continue in the same vein with medallions of fillet steak Braemar in whisky, cream and oatmeal, pheasant Glamis with cranberry, rosemary and a port wine sauce, or poached Fowey seatrout with a creamy smoked oyster sauce. Clootie dumpling (a Scottish fruit pudding) is worth choosing for dessert, or try the pancakes and special ice creams. A small but carefully chosen wine list accompanies the menu and there is an extensive selection of malt whiskies culled from the Highlands and Islands. Vegetarians catered for with advance notice. Access cards accepted.

Kea House

Licensed Restaurant

TREGONY
Nr TRURO, CORNWALL

Crossroads Motel, Scorrier, St Day, Cornwall
Tel: (0209) 820551

CROSSROADS MOTEL

Scorrier, Redruth.
Tel: (0209) 820551

Hours: *Open for coffee, lunch and dinner (last orders 9.30pm Mon–Thurs, 10pm Fri/Sat). Bar meals lunchtime.*

Average Prices: *A la Carte £13.50; Table d'Hôte £8.75; Sun lunch £5.50; snacks from £1.*

Wines: *House wine £5 per bottle.*

The Crossroads Motel can justly claim to lie at the very heart of Cornwall, equidistant from the cathedral city of Truro, the shipping port and yachting centre of Falmouth and the popular holiday resort of Newquay. The motel is modern both in its architecture and approach. The needs of the 1980's and, in particular, the burgeoning demand for elaborate conference facilities, are well catered for. A new wing of executive bedrooms has recently been added, for example, to complement the existing facilities, which can cater for up to 200 people.

The restaurant itself blends together the colours of pink and jade, both attractively set off by the dark oak beaming and furnishings. Lantern lighting completes the effect. However, far from the usual run of the mill hotel food, Crossroads is renowned for its cuisine, expertly created by chef Martin Churchill who was the runner-up for the 1987 Young Chef of the Year award.

Martin specialises in sauces, bringing to life ordinary dishes in new and original ways. On the starter list, for instance, a variety of sauces are available with Cornish crab, and there is also scallop of local seafood in a white wine sauce. Dishes available as a main course include roast loin of lamb stuffed with mushroom farce, supreme of chicken with an avocado mousse, vol au vent of kidneys in a Madeira sauce and roast duckling with black cherries and kirsch. For vegetarians, there is a roulade of cheese, served with a blackberry sauce. A good cross-selection of wines accompanies the meal with, for example, Chablis, Côte de Beaune and Châteauneuf-du-Pape, and, on Fridays, a resident pianist plays.
For a less formal alternative, the Celtic Bar, also decorated in shades of jade, serves filling bar snacks.

*Kingsclere Publications produces a varied list of publications in the **Where to Eat** series which cover areas as far apart as Scotland, The Channel Islands and Ireland.*

PENNYPOTS

Blackwater, Truro. Tel: (0209) 820347
Hours: Open for dinner Tues–Sat.
Average Prices   A la Carte £15. House wine £5 per bottle.

Competing at the World Culinary Olympics in Frankfurt late in 1988, Kevin Viner, a member of the gold medal winning team, also won an individual gold for his pastillage statue of Charlie Chaplin, which now stands in the reception area of his new restaurant, Pennypots. Kevin, who was also a runner-up in the Young Chef of the Year Award, is particularly interested in pastry and sugar work, and he hopes to give demonstrations on special evenings throughout the year. His cooking, as a general rule, is spontaneous, creating dishes with strong natural flavours from available local produce. The Pennypots' steak (stuffed with pâté, mushrooms, onions and herbs, cooked in garlic butter, and garnished with bacon and flaked almonds with a Madeira sauce), is just one example. Desserts naturally feature strongly and always available is his chocolate temptation (a chocolate, orange and Grand Marnier cream cheese on an almond chocolate biscuit with a black cherry sauce). The restaurant, housed in a 200-year-old building, is decorated in pink and grey and has a large pot sitting in one corner, into which, Jane (Kevin's wife), will drop a penny for every customer. When the pot is full, the money will be given to charity.

PENNYPOTS RESTAURANT

Chef Proprietor
Kevin Viner
Member of the
British Culinary
Olympic Team

Gold Medal Winner '88

British Team of Chefs

BLACKWATER · OLD A30 · NEAR TRURO · 0209 820347

THE DINING GALLERIES at the Penventon Hotel

Redruth. Tel: (0209) 214141

Hours: *Open for lunch and dinner.*

Average Prices: A la Carte £10.50; Table d'Hôte lunch £6.50; dinner £7.95

'The Flavour of Italy', 'The Best of France' and 'Britain's Heritage', are three of the menu headings at The Dining Galleries, emcompassing a wide range of dishes at reasonable prices. This is remarkable considering the surroundings. Delicate flower arrangements, attractively folded napkins and silver service compete for diners' attention. They are set against a backdrop of Venetian chandeliers in Murano glass, oil paintings and graceful tapestries, combining together in a skilful blend of style and elegance. The cuisine is unfussy, but well prepared. On the Italian menu, begin with melon garnished with almonds in amaretto, followed by pollo San Marco (chicken breasts in a creamy sauce flambéd at the table), and, on the French menu, a platter of Mediterranean shellfish and then filet de boeuf en croûte (fillet steak topped with pâté and Madeira in a puff pastry case). The English menu is the most varied, with steak Diane, duckling with fresh apple, chicken curry, lobster thermidor and more. This is a meal with all the trimmings — the last cup of coffee savoured whilst listening to the grand piano. For those who partake of too much liqueur gâteau, the hotel's Aphrodite health spa is the place to head for!

REDRUTH · CORNWALL
AA ★ ★ ★ **RAC**

Cornish Pixies? (Courtesy of Sue Morgan)

BASSET COUNT HOUSE

Carnkie, Redruth. Tel: (0209) 215181

Hours: *Open for lunch and dinner. Closed Mon. Bar meals lunchtime except Sun.*

Average Prices: *A la Carte £15; Sun lunch £6.95.*

Wines: *House wine £5.95 per bottle.*

The Basset Count House, a beautifully renovated, large granite building, once the accounts office of the famous Basset mine, now houses a cocktail bar, a lounge bar serving light lunches and a restaurant specialising in traditional Anglo-French dishes, prepared with fresh local produce. The menu is, therefore, seasonally based, but changed weekly. Melon with a blackcurrant sorbet and tropical fruits, or lobster tails in a mustard and brandy sauce, are typical offerings from the selection of starters. For the main course, there are dishes such as roast partridge with an apple and redcurrant sauce, sea bass en papillote with dill and peppers, roast breast of duck with a raspberry sauce and fillet steak with a port and Stilton sauce. Dishes are underscored by the refinement of the setting where delicate china and glassware grace the tables and antique furnishings provide a backdrop. Vegetarian dishes are also available on request. In addition to the fine selection of house wines, there is an interesting and extensive wine list.

The Basset Count House

Carnkie Redruth

THE LOWENAC

Basset Road, Camborne. Tel: (0209) 719295/6
Hours: *Open for lunch and dinner.*
Average Prices: *A la Carte £13.50; carvery £9.95.*
Wines: *From £4.15.*

Many of the mansion houses scattered throughout Camborne-Redruth were built on wealth acquired from the prosperous 19th century copper mines. But although the industry may have declined this century, the elegant residences still remain, a testament to former greatness. The Lowenac is one such house, moving with the times to cater now for the needs of the 1980's. The hotel prides itself on its conference facilities — in particular its separate conference room with en suite facilities such as a cocktail bar and Prestel television. The dining room serves an à la carte menu throughout the week and has a carvery on Fri/Sat. Both options depend upon seasonal availability and the à la carte changes every four to six weeks. Starters include Lowenac stuffed mushrooms (with garlic pâté, breadcrumbed and lightly fried) and French towt (courgettes topped with crab, mushrooms and cheese). For the main course there are dishes such as lemon sole Celestine (stuffed with crab, grapefruit and mushrooms in a rich Cointreau cream sauce), pork Marnier (sautéed in Grand Marnier and topped with spinach and almond), and the ever popular chateaubriand. Desserts covered with a generous layer of clotted cream conclude.

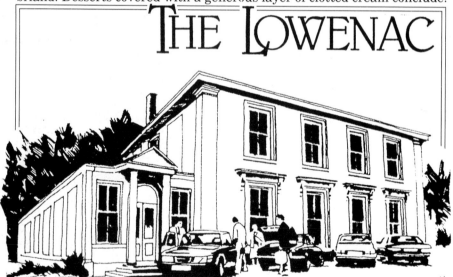

THE LOWENAC

BASSET ROAD, CAMBORNE   TEL: (0209) 719295 / 6

Peckish in Perth?

Hungry in Holyhead?

Famished in Felixstowe?

Ravenous in Roscommon?

■ WHERE TO EAT ■

The discerning diner's guide to restaurants throughout Britain and Ireland

Copies available from bookshops or direct from the publishers
Kingsclere Publications Ltd
Use the Order Form overleaf

ORDER FORM

To:
KINGSCLERE PUBLICATIONS LTD.
Highfield House, 2 Highfield Avenue, Newbury, Berkshire, RG14 5DS

Please send me

____ copies of *WHERE TO EAT in BERKSHIRE* @ £1.95 £ ____

____ copies of *WHERE TO EAT in BRISTOL, BATH & AVON* @ £2.50 £ ____

____ copies of *WHERE TO EAT in CORNWALL* @ £1.95 £ ____

____ copies of *WHERE TO EAT in CUMBRIA & THE LAKE DISTRICT* @ £1.95 £ ____

____ copies of *WHERE TO EAT in DORSET* @ £1.95 £ ____

____ copies of *WHERE TO EAT in EAST ANGLIA* @ £2.95 £ ____

____ copies of *WHERE TO EAT in EAST MIDLANDS* @ £1.95 £ ____

____ copies of *WHERE TO EAT in GLOS & THE COTSWOLDS* @ £1.95 £ ____

____ copies of *WHERE TO EAT in GUERNSEY* @ £0.80 £ ____

____ copies of *WHERE TO EAT in HAMPSHIRE* @ £1.95 £ ____

____ copies of *WHERE TO EAT in HERTS, BUCKS & BEDS* @ £2.50 £ ____

____ copies of *WHERE TO EAT in IRELAND* @ £1.75 £ ____

____ copies of *WHERE TO EAT in JERSEY* @ £0.80 £ ____

____ copies of *WHERE TO EAT in KENT* @ £2.95 £ ____

____ copies of *WHERE TO EAT in NORTH EAST ENGLAND* @ £1.95 £ ____

____ copies of *WHERE TO EAT in OXFORD & OXFORDSHIRE* @ £1.95 £ ____

____ copies of *WHERE TO EAT in SCOTLAND* @ £1.95 £ ____

____ copies of *WHERE TO EAT in SOMERSET* @ £1.50 £ ____

____ copies of *WHERE TO EAT in SURREY* @ £1.95 £ ____

____ copies of *WHERE TO EAT in SUSSEX* @ £2.95 £ ____

____ copies of *WHERE TO EAT in WALES* @ £2.95 £ ____

____ copies of *WHERE TO EAT in WILTSHIRE* @ £1.95 £ ____

____ copies of *WHERE TO EAT in YORKS & HUMBERSIDE* @ £1.95 £ ____

p&p at £0.50 (single copy), £1 (2–5 copies), £2 (6 copies) £ ____

GRAND TOTAL £ ____

Name ....

Address ....

....

Post code .... Cheque enclosed for £ ....

Your help in answering the following would be appreciated:

(1) Did you buy this guide at a SHOP ☐ TOURIST OFFICE ☐ GARAGE ☐ OTHER ☐

(2) Are any of your favourite eating places *not* listed in this guide? If so, could you please supply names and locations ....

....

....

(C1)

NEW WORLD CHINESE RESTAURANT

Market Place, St Ives. Tel: (0736) 797341

Hours: *Open for lunch and dinner.*

Average Prices: A la Carte £8.50.

The New World Chinese Restaurant provides a mêlée of traditional Chinese cuisine. Since the start of 1988 Michael Wong has changed the style of cooking from chop suey to higher quality, more traditional Chinese food. Crispy aromatic duck and dim-sum dishes are two of the available choices from a very extensive menu.

新世界酒家

NEW WORLD CHINESE RESTAURANT
Cantonese, Peking & Szechuan Cuisine — Dim Sum Available
MARKET PLACE, ST IVES, CORNWALL. TEL: (0736) 797341

TREWELLARD ARMS HOTEL

Trewellard, Pendeen, near Penzance. Tel: (0736) 788634

Hours   *Open for coffee, lunch and dinner (last orders 9.30pm). Closed Tues. Bar meals.*

Average Prices   *A la Carte £11; snacks from £1.75.*

Situated in one of the most flourishing tin and copper mining areas of the 19th century, The Trewellard Arms has been converted from miners' cottages, though original timbering and pillars carved by the miners have been left intact. The emphasis today is on the food, a mixture of traditional French and English. Try coarse chicken liver pâté, followed by entrecôte hunter-style, or home-made steak and kidney pie.

TREWELLARD ARMS HOTEL

Trewellard, Pendeen, Nr. Penzance
Telephone: (0736) 788634

59

THE
PANDORA
INN

Restronguet Creek, Mylor Bridge, Falmouth
Tel: 0326 - 72678

THE PANDORA INN

Restronguet Creek, Mylor Bridge, Falmouth.
Tel: (0326) 72678

Hours: *Open for coffee, lunch, tea and dinner (last orders*
9.30pm). Bar meals lunchtimes and evenings.
Average Prices: A la Carte £13; snacks from 75p.
Wines: *House wine £5.70 per bottle (restaurant), £3.95 (bar).*

The intensive development of tourism in Cornwall during the last few decades has dissipated much of the atmosphere which the tourists come in droves to experience. Tiny fishing villages which once barely supported their existing populations are yearly inundated by holiday-makers, but there are still pockets of Cornwall where the past almost seems to live on. Restronguet, a remote hamlet overhung by dense woodland on three sides and a small creek on the fourth, is one such place. Until the turn of the century, it was part of a ferry route through the Carrick Roads from Truro to Falmouth, and, even today, about half its summer visitors arrive by water. The Pandora Inn, bordering the waters of the creek, is the village's focal point. Its distinctive thatched and whitewashed exterior, envelops a Medieval interior, where low beaming and huge flagstones partner the open fireplace (situated halfway up the walls in case of flooding). Although dating back to the 13th century, the inn is named after its 18th century owner, Captain Edwards, who was commissioned to search out the *Bounty* mutineers off Tahiti. His ship the *HMS Pandora* was wrecked on the Barrier Reef and the captain, having been court-martialled back in England, retired to Cornwall. However, what sets The Pandora apart from other picturesquely sited pubs is the quality of its cuisine, which rivals the setting in terms of attracting the customers. The restaurant is situated on the upper floor and serves a combination of French and traditional English dishes with an emphasis on seafood. Starters include the chef's special home-made pâté, blending chicken livers, bacon, herbs and brandy, and also baked mushrooms covered with goats' cheese and sprinkled with peppercorns. For the main course, there are dishes such as salmis of pheasant (a pot roast in a red wine sauce), poussin forestière (whole roasted chicken with a mushroom and bacon garnish), and seafood pancakes (filled with crab, prawns and scallops in a creamy mushroom sauce). Lobsters and oysters are also prepared with advance notice. Downstairs in the bar there is a large selection of real ales and bar meals. Seafood again features strongly, with dishes such as grilled mackerel in walnut butter and moules marinière. Filled jacket potatoes, children's meals, grills and sandwiches are also served. The last include choices such as the vegetarian (cream cheese, nuts, lettuce and cucumber) and the Pandora club. In the summer, there is no better place to appreciate both the setting and the food served at this inn than outside on its floating pontoon.

THE PRINCE OF WALES

Newtown St Martin, near Helston.
Tel: (032 623) 247

Hours:	*Open for morning coffee, lunch, afternoon tea and dinner (last orders 10.30pm).*
Average Prices:	*A la Carte £5.50; Sun lunch £4; snacks £1–4.*
Wines:	*£4.50 per litre; 90p per glass.*

Aptly named for the Duchy of Cornwall, The Prince of Wales is located in a designated area of outstanding natural beauty. Gorse and Cornish heather, which flourish in the Goonhilly Downs, are bordered by a sea famed for its shipwrecks and smuggling. Originally a farmhouse and still retaining its low beams and village atmosphere, The Prince of Wales is popular with locals and visitors alike. It offers generous portions of traditional pub food cooked with care. Begin with crunchy mushrooms in a garlic dip or pâté maison, and follow with chicken Kiev, lemon sole Cullamore or gammon steak with pineapple. The house speciality is the very large farmer's grill and also the range of steaks which include steak chasseur and steak Rossini. For dessert there's gâteau, chocolate nut sundae, fruit pie and if there's room, a liqueur coffee to finish. Children are welcomed and amply catered for with their own menu. There are even Heinz baby foods on offer. All produce is fresh, coming from a nearby holding.

Prince of Wales

Proprietors: Andrew & Janet Crook

Public House — Beer Garden — Restaurant
Car Park

NEWTOWN ST. MARTIN Nr. HELSTON CORNWALL	Telephone: Manaccan (032 623) 247

THE MELLANOWETH RESTAURANT

Gweek, Helston.
Tel: (032 622) 271
Hours: *Open for dinner except Sun. Closed Mon in winter.*
                    Barbecue lunches and crêperie summer only.
Average Prices: *A la Carte £15.*
Wines: *House wine £4.50.*

Mellanoweth translated from Cornish means new mill, providing the
setting for Colin and Hazel Funnells' recently refurbished restaurant,
which now also contains a crêperie and courtyard serving light lunches
and barbecues during the summer months. In the timbered 30-seater
dining room, guests are faced with an array of carefully prepared dishes.
Giant king prawns in garlic, or Camembert with a kiwi fruit sauce make
tasty starters. Main courses include fresh salmon poached in champagne,
beef Mellanoweth (a cream and sherry sauce with onions and green
peppercorns), nutty pork casserole with buttered noodles and scallop and
bacon Mornay. Vegetarians are catered for given prior notice, with dishes
such as nut and herb croquettes. Dining at The Mellanoweth is a pleasant
experience in peaceful surroundings. The village of Gweek is in one of the
most solitary areas of Cornwall, at the head of the Helford river on the
Lizard Point peninsula. There is also an interesting seal sanctuary close
by.

The Mellanoweth
Restaurant

Tel: Reservations
Mawgan (032622) 271

Gweek
Helston, Cornwall

MEUDON HOTEL AND RESTAURANT

Mawnan Smith, near Falmouth. Tel: (0326) 250541

Hours: *Open for coffee, lunch, tea and dinner (last orders 8.45pm). Closed Dec/Jan. Bar meals lunchtime.*

Average Prices: *A la Carte £26; Table d'Hôte (6 courses) £19; snacks £3.50. House wine £7 per bottle.*

The coastline between Falmouth and the Helford river is one of the most temperate areas of the British Isles, and, under the guardianship of the National Trust, has not been unduly developed. Meudon Hotel is classically styled within and surrounded by beautiful hanging gardens, designed by the 18th century landscaper 'Capability' Brown. The gulf stream which passes across this area of Cornwall encourages the growth of exotic and rare shrubs, all to be found within the gardens that are overlooked by the restaurant. Quality English and French dishes are served with a bias towards locally caught fish dishes. Smoked trout pâté with Pernod and lime, or peach salad with blue cheese dressing, can be found as starters, followed by fillet of brill with prawns and pineapple, roast leg of lamb with stuffed nectarines and a sherry sauce and scallops of monkfish thermidor. On the dessert menu, crème diplomat Geneva style and fresh fruit summer pudding are popular choices. Midday meals available from the bar show equal imagination, with avocado pear in a prawn and Marie Rose sauce and Spanish omelette.

Meudon Hotel

MAWNAN SMITH, NR. FALMOUTH, CORNWALL TR11 5HT. Tel: 0326 250541

THE FERRY BOAT INN

Helford Passage, Mawnan Smith. Tel: (0326) 250625
Hours: *Open for coffee, lunch, tea in summer and dinner.*
                Bar meals available.
Average Prices: A la Carte £11.50; Sun lunch £3.95; snacks from 70p.
Wines: *House wine £4 per bottle.*

The winding waterways of the Helford river, immortalised by Daphne du Maurier in *Frenchman's Creek*, attract countless yachts and those seeking the peace and seclusion of its wooded banks. The isolated Ferry Boat Inn can be reached by car from Mawnan Smith, or, more appropriately for its setting, across the water from Monks Passage. The interior of the bar is breezy, with French windows opening out onto the waterside terrace, whilst the dining room, with its light oak woodwork and port-holed door, resembles a ship's cabin. Dishes are traditional, with starters including Ferryman's mussels prepared to the secret house recipe and South Coast chowder (seafood, cream and white wine). From the main course, try, perhaps, the salmon soufflé (cooked in egg and served with a lobster sauce), fillet of sole Walewska (cooked in wine with a cheese and prawn sauce) and poussin piri piri (baby chicken served in a very hot chilli sauce). To drink, there is a selection of European wines and some traditional St Austell ales like the Prince's Ale, brewed to celebrate the 21st birthday of Prince Charles.

The Ferry Boat Inn

Helford Passage, Mawnan Smith, Nr Falmouth. Tel: (0326) 250625

BUDOCK VEAN GOLF AND COUNTRY HOUSE HOTEL

Mawnan Smith, Falmouth. Tel: (0326) 250288

Hours: *Open for coffee, lunch, tea and dinner. Restaurant closed Jan/Feb. Bar meals lunchtimes.*

Average Prices: *A la Carte £14; Sun lunch £7.50; snacks from £1.40.*

Wines: *House wine £6.50 per bottle.*

Standing on an ancient Celtic religious site, The Budock Vean itself dates back to the 18th century and retains the stylish elegance of the period. It is bordered by the Helford river and surrounded by landscaped gardens which include a challenging golf course, tennis and swimming facilities. The hotel's dining room has a spacious and almost Medieval air to it, enhanced by its elevated ceiling, supporting stone pillars, and the heraldry along its walls. Jacket and tie are requested for dinner, but the atmosphere is far from stuffy and the service is friendly. All dishes are imaginative and beautifully prepared. For a starter, try the crown of melon with exotic fruit, marinated in coconut rum, with a passion fruit sorbet, or Helford oysters on a bed of crushed ice with lemon and wholemeal bread. Following on to the main course, there is saddle of English lamb with an apricot and chestnut seasoning, mint sauce and redcurrant jelly, or perhaps a mêlée of seafish in a rich lobster, cream sauce with brandy, garnished with mange-tout and mushrooms. International vintages accompany.

THE NIGHTINGALES RESTAURANT
at The Greenbank Hotel

Harbourside, Falmouth. Tel: (0326) 312440

Hours:	*Open for coffee, lunch, afternoon tea and dinner.*
Average Prices:	*A la Carte £15; snacks from £1.25.*
Wines:	*From £5.95 per bottle.*

The Greenbank Hotel enjoys one of the best settings in which to appreciate the beauty of Falmouth and its sweeping, natural harbour. The port's greatest importance lay in the 18th century as a mail packet station, but, since the coming of the railway in the early 19th century, it has attracted visitors because of its mild climate, including Florence Nightingale, who stayed at the hotel, and after whom the restaurant is named. Guests dining at the restaurant have a wonderful vista of a deep blue sea and the many yachts at the open anchorage of Carrick Roads. Their choice of food is also wide and naturally includes many fish dishes like the unusual monkfish tails, flavoured with stem ginger in a dry Martini sauce, or fresh local scallops in a white wine and mushroom sauce. Meat dishes include chicken beurre Café de Paris (breast of chicken with a herb and spice butter, breadcrumbed and deep fried), fillet of pork dijonnaise (cooked with onion, mushroom, gherkin, mustard, brandy, white wine and cream), and, for vegetarians, dishes such as spinach pancakes. Friendly service accompanies the meal at this family run hotel.

Greenbank Hotel

view of Greenbank circa 1850

Harbourside   Falmouth

THE BOSLOWICK INN

Prislow Lane, Falmouth.
Tel: (0326) 312010
Hours: *Open for lunch and dinner (last orders 9.30pm).*
Bar meals lunchtimes and evenings.
Average Prices: Bar meals £2.50–6.50; Sun lunch £5.95; snacks from £1.

In the modern suburb of Prislow, The Boslowick Inn is one of the few remaining places to maintain strong ties with its past, most notably in the form of a friendly ghost, spotted by many customers on the elegant staircase. He may have lived at the 16th century manor house on which the present inn was built, or have been a crew member on one of the packet ships whose panelling now decorates the interior of the inn.

Real ales and traditional bar meals, from steaks to snacks, are available at all times and a traditional roast is served in the dining room every Sunday.

Two open fires always ensure a warm welcome for guests and The Boslowick Inn is very much family hostelry, offering also a pool and snooker leisure area as part of its fine facilities.

Prislow Lane, Falmouth   *Tel: (0326) 312010*

LA CUCINA

25 Arwenack Street, Falmouth. Tel: (0326) 311007

Hours: *Open for lunch and dinner (last orders 11pm).*
Average Prices: *A la Carte £15; light lunches £1–3.*
Wines: *£5.90 per carafe.*

The coastline of the Cornish Riviera, characterized by sandy coves, craggy headland, tiny fishing villages and an exceptionally mild climate, is very reminiscent of the Continental Riviera before it was swamped by tourists. Falmouth has clung on to tradition and is still dominated by Pendennis Castle, built by Henry VIII during the 1540's to ward off the French. What La Cucina transports from the Mediterranean is its style of cooking and taverna atmosphere. Starters like bresaola con carrino (air dried beef with a creamy cheese filling), and traditional pasta and steak dishes, are surpassed only by the weekly-changing specialities. These include the classic fegato alla veneziana (calves' liver fried with onions and sage), bocconcini di vitello ai sapori e funghi (veal braised with herbs, tomatoes, white wine and mushrooms), and filetto di pato Torres (duck marinated in Torres orange liqueur and sautéed in butter). Highlight of all is the Greek meze alla taverna, a dinner for two, consisting of 10–15 dishes for £19.95. The wine list is equally extensive, with a range of Spanish dessert wines and liqueurs from all over the world. Informality is the key here, and especially popular are the gourmet evenings.

LA CUCINA

FINE MEDITERRANEAN RESTAURANT

25 ARWENACK STREET, FALMOUTH. TEL: 0326 311007

SECRETS

6 Arwenack Street, Falmouth. Tel: (0326) 318585

Hours: *Open for morning coffee, lunch, afternoon tea and dinner (last orders 10pm). Closed Sunday.*

Average Prices: *A la Carte from £6; snacks from £1.*

A harbourside location is the setting for Secrets. Chef Stephen Field was trained in France and his influence can be seen in many of the modern French dishes including the sauté de boeuf Beaujolais and poulet roulé which he created himself. Daytime snacks — jacket potatoes and lasagne, for example — are popular, as are cream teas in the terrace garden.

SECRETS

COFFEE SHOP – RESTAURANT

FALMOUTH

THE SHIPWRIGHT'S ARMS

Helford, near Helston. Tel: (032 623) 235

Hours: *Open for coffee, lunch and dinner (last orders 9pm). Closed Sun/Mon evening out of season.*

Average Prices: *A la Carte £10.50; house wine £5.50 per bottle.*

This old, thatched inn can be found hidden amid woodland that surrounds a small creek off the Helford river. It is paradoxically both a tranquil and popular spot. Seafood features strongly on the menu with crab, scallops, monkfish, prawns and more, as well as char-grilled steaks and burgers served from the nightly barbecue during summer months. Home-made desserts include sticky meringues with clotted cream.

THE
SHIPWRIGHT'S
ARMS

HELFORD
VILLAGE

Tel: (032 623) 235

THE YARD BISTRO AT TRELOWARREN MANOR

Trelowarren, Mawgan, Helston. Tel: (032 622) 595

Hours: *Open for coffee, lunch and dinner (last orders 9pm, 10pm Fri/Sat). Closed Jan/Feb. Bar meals lunchtime.*

Average Prices: *Table d'Hôte £13.50; Sun lunch £4.75; snacks from £1.*

Wine: *House wine £5.25 per carafe.*

The creeks and inlets of the Helford river unfold onto a plethora of peaceful waterside clearings. But there are few sights more impressive than that of nearby 17th century Trelowarren Manor, seen from across the expansive lawn in front of the castellated house. Home to the powerful Vyvyan family, who came to prominence during the Civil War as masters of the Royalist mint, it has now opened its doors to craft and pottery exhibitions, as well as a restaurant, situated in the carriage house of the stable yard. Legend says that the Vyvyans, one of the few families to escape the doomed kingdom of Lyonesse, kept a horse permanently saddled in case the same should happen again. The Yard Bistro offers light lunches and an à la carte menu where the speciality is fish, presented in a selection of French, traditional and nouvelle cuisine dishes. Home pickled salmon in brandy and dill as a starter could be followed by guinea fowl with black peppers and then, perhaps, peaches in grenadine and almonds for dessert. Vegetables are grown in the grounds and the wines are good value, especially the Bordeaux, Château La France at a third of the usual price.

MULLION COVE HOTEL

Mullion Cove, near Helston. Tel: (0326) 240328

Hours:	*Open for morning coffee, lunch and dinner*
	(last orders 8.30pm). Closed Nov–Feb.
Average Prices:	*Table d'Hôte £12; Sun lunch £5.95; snacks from 80p.*
Wines:	*House wine £5 per bottle.*

Mullion Cove encapsulates all that visitors envisage about Cornwall. Jagged cliffs and a windswept headland overhang a secluded 19th century harbour, famous for the extent of its smuggling. The whole area is owned by the National Trust who have preserved its wild beauty. The hotel, perched high on the headland, looks right out to sea and has its own attractions. A tennis court, solar heated swimming pool and sauna are joined at low tide by a sandy cove, ideal for bathing in. A wide-ranging table d'hôte menu changes daily and lobster is always prepared to order given 24 hours' notice, so that Monty the local fisherman has time to catch it. Starters usually include soup, fruit juices and some form of egg dish, for example devilled. Main courses are traditional with coq au vin, roast leg of pork with apple sauce, roast topside of beef with horseradish sauce, fillet of ling Mornay and fillet of whiting caprice. Desserts from the trolley, cheese and biscuits and coffee and mints are the finishing touches. Home-made fresh produce is the order of the day, available also from the bar.

the Mullion Cove Hotel

Mullion. South Cornwall
Tel: (0326) 240 328

MOUNT'S BAY INN

Mullion, near Helston. Tel: (0326) 240221
Hours: Open for coffee and bar meals. Rest. evenings only.
Average Prices: A la Carte £10.85; snacks from 80p; wine £5.

Mullion lies between three attractive coves and in the centre of the village is the Mount's Bay Inn with its warm, friendly welcome. Within, choose, from the bar menu, home-made steak and kidney pie, filled jacket potatoes and many more tempting dishes, or, in The Mulliners Restaurant, such delights as pear surprise, followed by fresh haddock in cream or, for vegetarians, nut cutlets in black cherry sauce.

Mount's Bay
Inn

Mullion
Tel. (0326) 240221

Feeding time at the Seal Sanctuary, Gweek (Courtesy of Sue Morgan)

THE HARBOUR INN

Commercial Road, Porthleven, Helston.
Tel: (0326) 573876
Hours: *Open for coffee, lunch, tea and dinner (last orders*
         9.15pm). Bar meals lunchtimes and evenings.
Average Prices: *A la Carte £8.50; Sun lunch £4; snacks from 90p.*
Wines: *House wine £4 per bottle.*

Known by locals as 'The Commercial', even though it changed name over 50 years ago, The Harbour Inn has witnessed the comings and goings of this small seaport for many years. There is now a new separate restaurant area with glazed modern partitioning, but retaining many artefacts of old, with a ship's wheel, diver's helmet and the massive old supporting pillars from the original Porthleven baulk crane.

Many types of fish (including shark), are brought straight from the quay and are the specialities of the restaurant's traditional menu, although you'll probably not experience anything like the six foot long royal sturgeon landed in 1983, or the two feet eight inches lobster caught in 1955! Dave and Wendy, the managers, also provide steaks and other meat dishes with children choosing from a 'Sprat's Corner' choice of pizzas, burgers, sausages and steakwiches. Bar food includes favourites like hot Cornish pasty, chicken and bacon pie, filled jacket potatoes and assorted ploughman's lunches. There are also eight en suite rooms and real ales.

The
HARBOUR
INN

PORTHLEVEN · CORNWALL
Telephone:
Management: Helston 573876
Visitors: Helston 573424

St. Austell Brewery
Independent Family Brewers
Est. 1851

THE QUEENS HOTEL

The Promenade, Penzance. Tel: (0736) 62371

Hours: *Open for Table d'Hôte bar lunch and dinner (last orders 8.45pm). No bar meals Sat/Sun.*

Average Prices: *Table d'Hôte £14; Sun lunch £8.50; buffet lunch £3.25.*

The Queens Hotel is an elegant, spacious hotel beautifully decorated with artefacts from the Newlyn School. Standing on the Promenade, the views from the restaurant across Mount's Bay are spectacular and the elegance of this Victorian hotel is reflected in the dining room. Tables are laid with quality linen and silver and dishes freshly prepared from local produce.

RICHMONDS RESTAURANT AND PATISSERIE

12–13 Chapel Street, Penzance. Tel: (0736) 63540

Hours:	*Open for coffee, lunch, tea and dinner.*
Average Prices	*A la Carte from £9.*
Wines	*House wine £5.95 per litre.*

Atmospherically and individually styled to recreate the feel of the '30's and '40's, when big band music had its heyday, Richmonds is a popular haunt both for its ambience and its cookery. Its wide Continental selection encompasses light and full à la carte meals, as well as a range of rich desserts. Starters include prawns in a garlic, tarragon and cream sauce with French bread, and the special Richmonds savoury peach stuffed with cheese and herb pâté with a cheese topping and served on a croûton. For the main course try fillet steak with mushroom and chicken pâté, wrapped and baked in puff pastry and served with a Madeira sauce. But always leave room for the desserts, the restaurant's speciality. Here there is chocolate and almond liqueur cake, hot apple tart coloche, a range of sundaes, Pavlovas and ice creams topped with sauces such as butterscotch and raspberry, and other desserts supplemented by a blackboard. Another popular feature is the Victorian breakfast served on the first Sunday of every month with Scotch porridge, smoked haddock and walnut bread toast with home-made strawberry jam.

THE GANGES

18 Chapel Street, Penzance. Tel: (0736) 65052

Hours: *Open for lunch and dinner*
                   (last orders 11.15pm Sun-Thurs, 11.45pm Fri/Sat).

Average Prices   *A la Carte £12.15.*

Wines: *House wine £5.75 per bottle.*

Mr E H Laskar, the owner of a chain of Ganges restaurants throughout Cornwall, has had many years' experience in the catering trade, in which time he has built up a reputation for providing classic Indian cuisine, well presented in attractive, but authentic surroundings. In the Ganges, Penzance, for example, there are a number of interesting chef's specialities. These include chicken jal ferezi (diced chicken grilled over a clay oven and then cooked with tomatoes and green peppers in an iron karahi), murug makhni (barbecued chicken tossed in butter with yoghurt, fresh cream and served in an exotic sauce), and the popular tandoori king prawn masala (charcoal grilled king prawn cooked in oriental spices with cream and butter to a secret house recipe). Curries also feature with mild kormas, cooked with cream and coconut, medium hot Malayas, cooked with pineapple, and the hot dhansaks, cooked with lentils.

The Ganges Indian Restaurant, 18 Chapel Street, Penzance. Tel: (0736) 65052

THE BERKELEY RESTAURANT AND CLUB ZERO

Abbey Street, Penzance. Tel: (0736) 62541
Hours: *Open for lunch and dinner. Rest. closed Sun.*
Average Prices: A la Carte £11.50; house wine £5.

The Berkeley Restaurant, with its neo art décor of the 1930's, almost takes a step back in time, and the same can be said of the tunnelled club below, where diners can follow a meal by dancing until 1am. English and Italian dishes feature on the menu, with breast of chicken in a creamy sauce with mushrooms and lemon juice, and pepperonata con formaggio al forno for vegetarians (aubergines, pimentos and onions topped with cheese).

CLUB ZERO
BERKELEY RESTAURANT

PENZANCE   TEL: (0736) 62541

RESTAURANT

46 NEW STREET
PENZANCE
CORNWALL

Dinner from 7 pm
Reservations:
Penzance (0736) 64408

Hours: *Open for lunch and dinner (last bookings 10pm).*
Closed Sun/Mon in winter.
Average Prices: A la Carte £16–20; light lunches £3–8.

Harris's is a popular and well run restaurant, with a pink and ivory décor and a wrought iron staircase leading to the lounge bar, where light lunches are served. The menu is innovative, but deliberately simple. Watercress and lettuce soup could be followed by fish, like John Dory in a cream, wine and tarragon sauce in summer, and game in winter. Desserts like lemon soufflé in a dark chocolate case are a finishing touch.

ENZO

Newbridge, Penzance.
Tel: (0736) 63777

Hours: Open for dinner (last orders 9.30pm). Closed Thurs off season.

Average Prices: A la Carte £12.

Wines: House wine £4.80 per carafe; £6 per litre.

Enzo prides itself not only on an interesting menu, but also on its unusual surroundings. The restaurant is situated in a conservatory overflowing with exotic plants and flowers. The open-plan layout also means that diners can watch the preparation of their meals. The antipasti trolley, loaded with a selection of seafood, meat or vegetarian hors d'oeuvre, makes a good start to the meal. There are also other choices with, for example, melanzane ripiene (hot aubergine stuffed with Mozzarella and ham in a tomato sauce), or lumache alla piemontese (snails in a tomato, sweet pepper and garlic sauce served on lightly fried bread). The main course comprises fish, pasta and meat dishes including cochiglie all'Enzo (fresh local scallops with apple, artichoke, cream and mushrooms on spaghetti), spaghetti all' arrabbiata (tomato, onion, bacon, garlic and chilli sauce), and pollo vesuviano (crumbed escalope topped with Mozzarella, tomato sauce and asparagus). For dessert, the selection is also totally fresh and home-made, with tiramisu a speciality.

Enzo Restaurant, Newbridge, Penzance   (0736) 63777

Postscript

The sun shines on Cornwall in more than one way. The wealth of good, fresh, traditional fare available in the county was discussed as a prelude to this guide, but it is worth dwelling once more upon the Cornish riches revealed in the pages which followed. The individuality of its eating places is second to none. They range from country mansions to homely little inns, each rich in its own character and many with tales to tell.

PAST GLORIES

Flick through the pages and read again about the ghosts of The Boslowick Inn or The Edgcumbe Arms at Cremyll, or the luxurious Budock Vean Hotel, built on an ancient Celtic religious site. The Carpenters Arms at Metherell was built to house the craftsmen building Cotehele Manor in the 15th century, but even older is The Old Rectory at St Columb, constructed in 1288, resplendent with stained glass and surrounded by a moat! Indeed, historians can enjoy a real field day locating centuries-old smugglers' haunts, as well as an ancestral home belonging to a family with Civil War connections, and then working out which inn claims to be the oldest coaching house in North Cornwall. Find out also which inn played host to Florence Nightingale, which is named after the ship used to track down The Bounty mutineers and where a Poet Laureate rests in peace.

INTERNATIONAL IDEAS

There's a cosmopolitan Cornwall too, hidden in the pages of *Where to Eat*. Indulge yourself on Continental cooking at many of the fine establishments listed — French, for example, at The Royal Oak in Lostwithiel, Treglos Hotel near Padstow or Falmouth's Secrets. The Mellanoweth has a crêperie, whilst Enzo's Italian recipes are another option. La Cucina draws its inspiration from the Mediterranean in general, and the meze is a real highlight. Anna Harris is the Polish-born chef at Headlands but a glance at the menu reveals internationalism in the form of dishes like teriyaki steaks. Alternatively, visit the bar of The Falcon at Falconbridge for spicy Mexican dishes, whilst Italy, France and Britain all have their own menus at The Penventon Hotel in Redruth and the chef at The Trewithen Restaurant, again in Lostwithiel, has worked in Bali and

New Zealand, not to mention the Black Forest where he learned more than gâteau-making. Closer to home, there's warm Scottish hospitality at Kea House, and seafood is so fresh at Mullion Cove that Monty, the fisherman, needs 24 hours' notice to catch it, although it's unlikely he'll turn up a 2ft 8ins lobster as was once caught at The Harbour Inn in Porthleven. For the youngest diners, The Prince of Wales at Newtown St Martin even serves baby foods!

ATMOSPHERICS

Of course, there's more to dining out than the food, important though it is. Atmosphere can make or break an evening and unusual décor often helps conjure an ambience. The Chart Room at Fowey lines its walls with fascinating old maps, and a collection of postage stamps adds to the interest in a former post office, now appropriately called Stamps. At Janners in Wadebridge jazz instruments are a talking point, whilst, in Penzance, characterful décor from the '30s holds sway at The Berkeley Restaurant and artefacts from the Newlyn School of artists abound at The Queens. Out of doors, when the weather smiles, relax on the waterside terrace of The Ferry Boat Inn, or feast the eye at Meudon Hotel on gardens sculpted by 'Capability' Brown.

TRIVIAL PURSUITS

Finally, a few more posers. Did you spot the inn with magical dishes on the menu? Or where a resident pianist plays on a Friday night? Rediscover the restaurant named after mountains in Morocco, and where you can take your choice from no less than 19,600 different sandwiches. It'll show you yet again just how bountiful Cornwall is. May the sun continue to shine!

Glossary

To assist readers in making the sometimes confusing choice from the menu, we have listed some of the most popular dishes from restaurants featured in *Where to Eat* up and down the country, together with a brief, general explanation of each item. Of course, this can never be a comprehensive listing — regional trends result in variation in the preparation of each dish, and there's no accounting for the flair and versatility of the chef — but we hope it offers readers a useful guideline to those enigmatic menu items.

STARTERS

Foie gras .... duck or goose liver, often made into pâté
Gazpacho .... a chilled Spanish soup of onion, tomato, pepper and cucumber
Gravad lax .... raw salmon marinated in dill, pepper, salt and sugar
Guacamole .... a creamy paste of avocado flavoured with coriander and garlic
Hummus ..... a tangy paste of crushed chick peas flavoured with garlic and lemon
Meze .... a variety of spiced Greek hors d'oeuvre
Moules marinière .... mussels in a sauce of white wine and onions
Samosa .... small pastry parcels of spiced meat or vegetables
Satay .... small skewers of grilled meat served with a spicy peanut dip
Taramasalata .... a creamy, pink paste of fish roe
Tzatziki .... yoghurt with cucumber and garlic
Vichyssoise .... a thick, creamy leek and potato soup, served cold

FISH

Bouillabaisse .... chunky fish stew from the south of France

Coquilles St Jacques .... scallops
Lobster Newburg .... with cream, stock and, sometimes, sherry
Lobster thermidor .... served in the shell with a cream and mustard sauce, glazed in the oven
Sole Walewska .... a rich dish of poached fish in a Mornay sauce with lobster
Sole bonne femme .... cooked with stock, dry white wine, parsley and butter
Sole véronique .... poached in a wine sauce with grapes
Trout meunière .... floured, fried and topped with butter, parsley and lemon

MAIN COURSES

Beef Stroganoff .... strips of fillet steak sautéed and served in a sauce of wine and cream
Beef Wellington .... beef in a pastry crust
Boeuf Bourguignon .... steak braised in a red wine sauce with onions, bacon and mushrooms
Chateaubriand .... thick slice of very tender fillet steak
Chicken à la King .... pieces of chicken in a creamy sauce
Chicken Kiev .... crumbed breast filled with herb butter, often garlic
Chicken Marengo .... with tomato, white wine and garlic
Chicken Maryland ..... fried and served with bacon, corn fritters and fried banana
Osso buco .... knuckle of veal cooked with white wine, tomato and onion
Pork Normandy .... with cider, cream and calvados
Ris de veau .... calves' sweetbreads
Saltimbocca alla romana .... veal topped with ham, cooked with sage and white wine

Steak au poivre .... steak in a pepper and wine sauce
Steak bordelaise .... steak in a red wine sauce with bone marrow
Steak Diane .... steak in a peppered, creamy sauce
Steak tartare .... raw, minced steak served with egg yolk
Tournedos Rossini ...... fillet steak on a croûton, topped with foie gras and truffles
Wiener Schnitzel .... escalope of veal, breadcrumbed and fried

SAUCES

Aioli .... strong garlic mayonnaise
Anglaise .... thick white sauce of stock mixed with egg yolks, lemon and pepper
Arrabbiata .... tomatoes, garlic and hot peppers
Béarnaise .... thick sauce of egg yolks, vinegar, shallots, white wine and butter
Carbonara .... bacon, egg and Parmesan cheese
Chasseur .... mushrooms, tomatoes, shallots and white wine
Dijonnaise .... cold sauce of eggs and mustard, similar to mayonnaise
Hollandaise .... egg yolks and clarified butter
Mornay .... creamy sauce of milk and egg yolks flavoured with Gruyère cheese
Pesto .... basil, marjoram, parsley, garlic, oil and Parmesan cheese
Pizzaiola .... tomatoes, herbs, garlic and pepper
Provençale .... tomato, garlic, onion and white wine
Reform .... pepper and white wine with boiled egg whites, gherkins and mushrooms
Rémoulade .... mayonnaise with mustard, capers, gherkins and herbs, served cold

DESSERTS

Banoffi pie .... with toffee and banana
Bavarois .... cold custard with whipped cream and, usually, fruit
Crème brûlée .... caramel-topped, rich vanilla flavoured cream
Crêpes Suzette .... pancakes flavoured with orange or tangerine liqueur
Parfait .... chilled dessert with fresh cream
Pavé .... square shaped light sponge
Pavlova .... meringue-based fruit dessert
Sabayon/zabaglione .... whisked egg yolks, wine and sugar
Syllabub .... whipped cream, wine and sherry
Zuccotto .... a dome of liqueur-soaked sponge filled with fruit and cream
Zuppa inglese .... an Italian trifle

CULINARY TERMS

Coulis .... a thin purée of cooked vegetables or fruit
Croustade .... a case of pastry, bread or baked potato which can be filled
Devilled .... seasoned and spicy, often with mustard or cayenne
Dim-sum .... various Chinese savoury pastries and dumplings
Duxelles .... stuffing of chopped mushrooms and shallots
En croûte .... in a pastry or bread case
Farce .... a delicate stuffing
Feuilleté .... filled slice of puff pastry
Florentine .... containing spinach
Goujons .... thin strips of fish
Julienne .... cut into thin slices
Magret .... a cut from the breast of a duck
Mille-feuille .... thin layers of filled puff pastry
Quenelles .... spiced fish or meat balls
Roulade .... stuffed and rolled
Sauté .... to brown in oil
Tournedos .... small slice of thick fillet

Index

ALPHABETICAL INDEX TO ESTABLISHMENTS

ALPHABETICAL INDEX TO TOWNS AND VILLAGES